Tethered Money

Managing Digital Currency Transactions

Tethered Money
Managing Digital Currency Transactions

Gideon Samid

AMSTERDAM • BOSTON • HEIDELBERG • LONDON
NEW YORK • OXFORD • PARIS • SAN DIEGO
SAN FRANCISCO • SINGAPORE • SYDNEY • TOKYO
Academic Press is an Imprint of Elsevier

Academic Press is an imprint of Elsevier
125, London Wall, EC2Y 5AS, UK
525 B Street, Suite 1800, San Diego, CA 92101-4495, USA
225 Wyman Street, Waltham, MA 02451, USA
The Boulevard, Langford Lane, Kidlington, Oxford OX5 1GB, UK

Notices
Knowledge and best practice in this field are constantly changing. As new research and experience broaden our understanding, changes in research methods, professional practices, or medical treatment may become necessary.

Practitioners and researchers must always rely on their own experience and knowledge in evaluating and using any information, methods, compounds, or experiments described herein. In using such information or methods they should be mindful of their own safety and the safety of others, including parties for whom they have a professional responsibility.

To the fullest extent of the law, neither the Publisher nor the authors, contributors, or editors, assume any liability for any injury and/or damage to persons or property as a matter of products liability, negligence or otherwise, or from any use or operation of any methods, products, instructions, or ideas contained in the material herein.

British Library Cataloguing-in-Publication Data
A catalogue record for this book is available from the British Library

Library of Congress Cataloging-in-Publication Data
A catalog record for this book is available from the Library of Congress

ISBN: 978-0-12-803477-4

For information on all Academic Press publications
visit our website at http://store.elsevier.com/

Typeset by Thomson Digital
Printed and bound in the United States

Working together
to grow libraries in
developing countries

www.elsevier.com • www.bookaid.org

Dedication

Dedicated to My Father Ya'acov Samid
Who graced me with his love and wisdom,
distilled in his 102 years on this earth.
Crediting his longevity to his
ever-present curiosity.

Contents

4.   Anatomy of Digital Money Products

Purpose

From the hidden basements of modern cryptography emerged a technology that offers to represent money without any physical manifestation – just a string of bits. Such bit money (crypto money, digital money) can be stored, transacted, secured, and leveraged in ways so revolutionary that the full impact of this new formation of money will be unfolded by people too young to be imprinted by how we pay and bank today. The purpose of this book is to introduce this new money innovation, and to emphasize what shapes up to be its most potent first wave advantage: tethered money.

Money today is universal – it buys anything priced for its face value. Once it is handed over, its recipient is its master, which is just and good for money earned in good faith. Alas, in our modern economy a growing portion of the micro- and macrofinancial transactions involves unearned money: money received not against an equal measure of goods and services but rather on expectations, and on considerations rooted in the future. Such are: grants, endowments, welfare checks, and, of course, the massive credit market where money is handed over at risk. Since money today is universal, the recipient of such unearned money may readily deviate from the terms of the transaction and use this money in ways inconsistent with the purpose for which the giver has entered into the deal. This prospect discourages givers and payers on one hand, and opens the door for recipients' fraud, waste and abuse, on the other. Both consequences arrest progress and inhibit prosperity. Say then: should we succeed in deuniversalizing money, we will reap the benefit of accelerated progress and early blooming prosperity. The good news is that tethered money – money fused to its intended purpose – is a technological reality today, and what is needed is to adopt this technology in micro- and macroeconomics so that its immense power will be unleashed.

Prologue

All the great inventions of humanity were made possible because of the division of labor; allowing their inventors to have food and shelter without having to spend their time in agriculture and construction. Division of labor was enabled by the universal human invention: money. Money allows each of us to focus on what we do best, and thereby to uplift society as a whole. But money has also become a frightfully effective means to control society, for good or for ill. And hence society should be most concerned with how money is created and how it moves about.

Money is the way people express their will and preference; the way people are motivated and rewarded. More money is everybody's goal; some would use violence and crime to attain it. Money is inherently unstable. Money is dysfunctional if it is concentrated in the hands of the very few, and it is ineffective if it is forcibly distributed to attain universal equality of wealth. What is the ideal distribution?

Society's interests may, arguably, be stated as: money should be in the hands of those who have the talent and ability to make the most societal good out of it, but also in the hands of its most deserving members. Society, therefore, has an urgent need to keep the distribution of money aligned with the distribution of human talent, and consistent with human sense of morality.

An important tool to help achieve this societal objective has recently been offered by the new technology of tethered money: a means to shed light on the dynamics of money, and control its flow according to the interests of its ultimate owner: the society that has established the prevailing currency that its count represents transactional value – societal wealth.

Roadmap

Following an extensive *Introduction* to the concepts of digital money and tethered money, the reader is guided to Chapter 1 "Money: An Irreverent Analysis" an uncommon take on the issue of money and its role in society; how central banks wrestle with unpredictability, explaining why we should pay utmost attention to manage and track money, navigating between transparency and privacy. The remarkable notion of tethered money is discussed and illustrated. Chapter 2 "Tethered Money: Use and Impact" describes some of the myriad of applications of tethered money, and how it impacts society toward a more efficient and moral living, with less financial waste, decreased level of fraud, and minimized abuse. This chapter makes it clear why we should put forth the effort needed to use modern crypto technology to make tethered money a reality. Chapter 3 "Digital Money: The Security Nightmare" brings to light the worrisome issue of cyber security: a flawed design might devolve into a global catastrophe. The chapter explains the vulnerabilities of digital money, the limitation of modern cryptography, how to mitigate the risk, and how to build a bold and effective digital money framework. The last chapter, Chapter 4 "Anatomy of Digital Money Products" delves into the prevailing categories of digital money, their main attributes, advantages, shortcomings, their competitive posture, and the prospective road ahead. The book concludes with a few relevant appendices.

Quotations

In the Colonies, we issue our own paper money. We call it Colonial Script, and we issue only enough to move all goods freely from the producers to the Consumers; and as we create our money, we control the purchasing power of money, and have no interest to pay.

There are three faithful friends – an old wife, an old dog, and ready money.

Benjamin Franklin

Anyone who lives within their means suffers from a lack of imagination.

Oscar Wilde

The various necessities of life are not easily carried about, and hence man agreed to employ in their dealings with each other something which was intrinsically useful and easily applicable to the purpose of life. For example, iron, silver, and the like. Of this the value was first measured by size and weight, but in the process of time they put a stamp upon it, to save the trouble of weighing and to mark value.

Aristotle

Do you remember back in the days when you thought that nothing could replace the dollar? Today, it practically has.

Ronald Reagan

The man who damns money has obtained it dishonorably; the man who respects it has earned it.

Ayn Rand

There's nothing in the world so demoralizing as money.

Sophocles

Don't think money does everything or you are going to end up doing everything for money.

In general, the art of government consists in taking as much money as possible from one class of citizens to give to the other.

Voltaire

Let all the learned say what they can, 'Tis ready money makes the man.

William Somerville

Money is like muck, not good except it be spread.

Francis Bacon

Coin is the sinew of war.

Francois Rabelais

The world is his, who has money to go over it.

Emerson

Money is like a sixth sense without which you cannot make a complete use of the other five.

Somerset Maugham

Whoever controls the volume of money in any country is absolute master of all industry and commerce. And when you realize that the entire system is so easily controlled, one way or another, by a few powerful men at the top, you will not have to be told how periods of inflation and depressions originate.

James A. Garfield

The U.S. government has a technology, called a printing press (or today, its electronic equivalent), that allows it to produce as many U.S. dollars as it wishes at no cost.

Ben Bernanke

In the absence of the gold standard, there is no way to protect savings from confiscation through inflation. There is no safe store of value.

Alan Greenspan

What's the subject of life – to get rich? All of those fellows out there getting rich could be dancing around the real subject of life.

Paul A. Volcker

In the main it will be found that a power over a man's support (salary) is a power over his will.

Alexander Hamilton

Introduction: Tethered Money – a Game Changer

What is possible now, and what was impossible yesterday is to disrupt the universality of money: to *deuniversalize* currency, to tether cash, to tie a payment to its intended purpose. And that's a very big deal.

Tethered money: stored value inexorably tied to its intended purpose, useless otherwise, is a feasible technological reality that can actually tweak the old invention – money – and jolt it to have a dramatic new impact on societal well being.

Air miles, gift cards, discount coupons – all are examples of tethered money. They function as money with a restricted use. If you planned to dine in at a particular restaurant, then the 40% discount coupon you use works as cash equivalent. Similarly for a flight you would have had to pay for, if you had not used your air miles. The entity that provided you with such tethered money retains control over its use, after having transferred it to your possession. This is in contrast to having given you the same amount in cash, against an unenforceable promise to use it as intended. This highlights the fact that nominal money comes untethered, with the freedom to use it for any purpose, for any goods or services priced for its face value. The seller will hardly bother himself with the question of where you got your cash from, who gave it to you, or for what purpose.

Walking into a shopping center, with a full wallet, a person himself may not have a clear idea as to how he will use his cash, what would he purchase this evening. Buyers walk in with a sense of power – they can purchase anything they fancy for the cash at hand. Worse, most of us walk around with a credit line, using our "plastic" up to our credit limit to buy anything and everything that is priced under our expenditure ceiling. Such is the power of possessing the currency of the land. Is there something wrong here?

This freedom of use is the joy and benefit of the money earner. Having provided goods, services, or efforts, and getting paid for it, you earned the freedom to dispose of your cash as you see fit – be whimsical, if you wish. Alas, our modern economy is built to a large degree on *unearned money* – money that was not attained against fair goods and services, but was rather secured as a loan, a credit, a grant, a charity, a welfare check, a payment advance – as part of a long-term plan for something specific to happen and benefit the money provider.

The problem is that such money can be used in the shopping mall as described above – freely, regardless of the use-intent articulated by the provider of such unearned money. A person may be granted a home construction loan secured by the progressive construction per se, but he or she may use the cash to purchase an expensive cruise travel; a businessperson may persuade his banker to loan him expansion money, but uses the funds to settle a personal debt; a welfare recipient may use his dollars in a liquor store, not in the grocery; a researcher may divert his grant money for personal travel; an insurance company is going high-risk with its premiums funds. These are all examples of a payer expecting the payee to do one thing with the paid money but the payee doing something different.

Tethered money, once we deploy the technology to accomplish it, will keep the payer in control of the handed-over money, and thereby will encourage many money owners to risk their money on a prospective future scenario. So while the tethered money will decrease the freedom and control of its possessor, this control is not lost but simply shifted to the source of that money. Arguably, the tethered money regimen is more just since the payee has not earned it against his goods, services, efforts or sweat, but rather received it by promising some action in the future, sometimes even less.

Money then will have a usage sphere, which may be as narrow as, say, air miles, usable only for flights on same airlines and under its prevailing limitations, subject to the imposed expiration date. Or it may be used for traveling on land, sea, or air, or perhaps it can be used for payment to any named city vendor. The tether – the leash – may be short or long, the restriction may be narrow or broad. Winning a double ticket to a specific show for a specific date is an example of narrowness, and using the money to pay anyone except Bob, is an example of broadness.

In a bad economy, business is sluggish, and there are fewer opportunities to earn money against one's goods, services, sweat and effort. When this happens the government flexes its muscles on countless initiatives that in essence amount to providing unearned money, cast as grants, unemployment checks, welfare, tax incentives, rebates, student loans, etc. If such money is indistinguishable from earned money then its payees will be more inclined to enhance its receipt rather than vie for earned cash. If such unearned payments will be tethered, then practically and psychologically they will count as less than untethered money, which its recipient had to exchange a needed valuable for. The freedom to use such money for anything that cost as much, will be much more appreciated. So tethered money will, on one hand, render the government initiatives more productive, and less abuse prone, and on the other hand it will not discourage people from seeking an earned money deal, to claim the untethered freedom to do with it as they please.

It's true that a payer of unearned money could in theory always demand an explicit contract that would limit the use of the money to be consistent with the intent of the payer. Alas, the money itself, once it has passed, is history-free, context-free, undisclosing as to its origin, or method of attainment. A nominal coin or paper bill is silent about its track record from the moment it was minted to the moment it is being paid. So, contract or not, the now money possessor will use it with total freedom. What then are the options of the contract holder in return? First, the payer will have to monitor and follow the money he transferred. Then, the payer will have to render judgment as to a prospective violation of the terms of the transaction, and after that he would have to alert and complain to the abusive recipient; argue, demand, insist, and at the end of this exhaustive effort the payer might be left with only choice: a lawsuit. Of course, this tedious action-path is not practical in view of the countless instances of unearned money payments. *The revolution of tethered money is that its very nature is such that its use is restricted; it cannot be abused or misused (by normal efforts). It is impossible to misdirect, or to violate its terms of payment – or nearly impossible.*

Remember the old travelers' checks? They were a form of tethered money restricted for paying to oneself. Only the named owner could use those checks to buy nominal (untethered) currency for its face value. And as a result, they provided security because, if lost or stolen, they would be replaced and the thief is left empty-handed: while he now has his victim's money, he does not have the victim's identity (identity theft notwithstanding). The new technology offers a modern version of these old travelers' checks. Cryptography will very easily tether money to its holder, providing a similar security. This alone will make it safe for people to keep their money in their phone, rather than in their bank; let's go a step further: *they will be able to use their cell phone as their banking establishment.* Similar security could be accomplished for financial institutions holding large sums of money. Today these huge amounts of capital are tracked through numbers, which carry a value, but no identity. A hacker that logs in as an "administrator" in the host computer will be able to change that number, and steal the balance, but if the same sum has been kept as tethered digital money, then stealing it will do the thief no good, and that is why it won't happen.

Air-miles, gift cards, coupons, and prizes today are the forbearers of broadly traded, widely leveraged, tethered money, through and across the entire economy, discouraging abuse, encouraging long range productive bidding.

The strategy for global prosperity is, without a doubt, a means to provide resources and power to the most talented and capable among us because these individuals will be in the best position to exploit such power and resources and build solutions to society's challenges. Alas, at any given moment, the distribution of wealth and resources substantially deviates from the distribution of talent and accomplishment ability. And hence, society needs to develop a mechanism to align these two distributions so that its most capable members will control a commensurate measure of its resources. Capitalism proposes one way to achieve that goal, and socialism proposed an opposite way, but both theories of economics do agree that a mechanism to provide the most talented among us with the resources to work with should be applied. Indeed, history has shown that when a rational credit system prevails, prosperity follows. Now, all credit payments exchange unearned money: money given against some future expectation. If the receiver of that money is subject to the temptation to abuse its original purpose, then the giver is held back by suspicion and apprehension. If, on the contrary, the payer is provided with clear assurances that his or her money will be used in ways consistent with the agreed-upon terms, then the payer/giver will be more inclined to risk his or her money in the credit market. More money will flow from those who have it, to those who can do the most with it. This is how a simple technological solution that assures the most desired disposition of money acts as a powerful accelerator for human progress. Healthy and robust credit market fueled by the technology of tethered money will push money to valuable research, will provide funds to daring leap-frog start-ups, will attract resources to large, long-term projects, will invest in multiyear programs for education, and cultural improvements.

In recent years we have witnessed accelerated productivity owing to the marvels of technology. Much fewer people take care of the same business that a threefold count of people had to attend to, only yesterday. Productivity is a boon to manufacturers, but a curse to the multitude that is being dropped out of the workforce. If they are too old they wouldn't be able to catch up with the newly skills, and, as a result, society, structurally, would find itself supporting a growing number of dependents. A growing measure of resources is diverted to unemployment compensation, to welfare, to educational programs, to retraining initiatives, etc. All this money is essentially unearned sums. It is given with a strict expectation of use limitation. The reality though is that the recipients of this kind of money may get tempted to dispose of it in ways inconsistent with the aim of the givers. As a result, the efficacy of the programs, under which such money is paid, suffers and neither society, nor the recipients get the best out of them. Here again, a simple effective cryptographic solution for tethered money will ensure that all those billions of dollars are funneled to the purpose for which they were designed.

Government raises taxes, amasses treasures, and then a small number of bureaucrats are given the authority to dispose of that treasure, all for the good of society. These faceless bureaucrats, in most cases, face a very compelling temptation to exploit their spending power. There is a huge gray area of abuse, way beyond the prosecutorial radar. Budgets are not earned, they are allotted, and spent with less than utmost care, at the very best, or in violation of the criminal code, at worst. Each government has its stories of massive corruption: human nature is what it is, not what our preachers and philosophers would wish it to be. Institutions that dispense of First World money to Third World recipients have thousand-nights-and-one stories of bold and daring abuse of various aid money – and no solution in sight. A solution is finally visible – tethered money – money that resists fraud, waste and abuse.

It is fascinating that an embryonic concept that for years has been limited to reward points and air-miles, can now be leveraged with advanced technology to become no less than the technological answer to fraud, waste, and abuse, and more importantly to become the leverage with which to catapult world economical reality into sustainable global prosperity.

Chapter 1

Money: An Irreverent Analysis

To understand the impact of tethered money, we need to remind ourselves how powerful, mysterious, and convoluted money is. On one hand, money is a universal invention repeated with few conceptual differences by all human societies everywhere, and credited with allowing society to evolve through division of labor. On the other hand, after five or even seven thousands of years of use experience, we are still debating what this invention is, how to measure it, how to handle it, and how to appraise it. Is money gold? Is money energy? Is money an illusion? Some serious thinkers claim each of the above. As much as we praise money and its clear societal benefits, we also castigate it as the "tool of the devil," the "root of sin." Let's touch base with the notion, the power, the thrill, the promise of money *per se*, and then sort out how money can be tethered and what does it mean.

MONEY: THE NUMERIC RESIDUE OF SOCIETY

Money is the numeric residue of society, its mirror, and its hammer. It is indispensable; it is mysterious, complex, and emotive. Its scarcity is depressing, its pursuit invigorating.

Tethered Money: Managing Digital Currency Transactions. http://dx.doi.org/10.1016/B978-0-12-803477-4.00001-6
1

Money is the rope that ties us to each other and renders individuals into a society. When that rope is pulled, the jolt reverberates. We vote daily with the disposition of our money. We pay for what alleviates our fear, provides for our necessities, or promotes our comfort, play, joy, and well being. For the gain of money, we fit ourselves into a limiting box, and with the power of money, we get ourselves out of the box.

Money has no intrinsic value; it's worthless for complete loners, stamps mutuality on strangers, pokes the mystery of trust, and engenders suspicion among close ones. Money fulfills its function well only if it maintains its buying power by measurably shrinking its supply when the economy shrinks and proportionally increasing its supply when the economy expands. Both inflation and deflation are self-fulfilling – posing a daunting difficulty on society as it tries to keep money stable. Money used to be passed on in exchange of equal value, or say, money used to be earned, but modern economies promote transactions wherein money is handed over as charity, endowment, welfare, chance expectations, or otherwise, not as an exchange that terminates when the money changes hands. This new reality further complicates the crisscross flow of money. The law of unintended consequences hits time and again, *harming anyone trying to manage that flow.*

Society exercises itself as a healthy entity by providing frictionless any-which-way flow of its currencies. Money must be stored, moved, and paid so efficiently that from the decision to the action, the process will be instantaneous, effortless, and, of course, secure and accountable. This can only be accomplished by moving forward boldly and promoting the expression of money to its ultimate state of versatility, mobility, handleability, and abstraction: *a string of binary digits – just a sequence of ones and zeros.*

We tried it before, but our approach was badly flawed. We used a clever formula that we knew is breakable; we employed an algorithm that was to last only until its hidden mathematical vulnerability is discovered. It is not a way to manage the numeric residue of society. Now we know better. We construct money as an open platform; we set up the underlying protocols and expect a wave of developers to fit the payment function into everyday's activity and transform banking into a global outreach, optimized risk, and credit regimen.

MONEY: MIGHTIER THAN THE SWORD

Social power is smartly exercised with money. Abusive power brokers ill steer the flow of currency, hide the source of their cash, conceal the track record of their wealth, misapply the treasures in their custody, circumvent the disposition of payments, muscle and abuse the economic leverage of loans, grants, and credit, and ruthlessly procure and purchase that which should never be bought with money.

The genius of money as a weapon is in its nonviolent appearance, in one's ability to exercise it brutally without raising the full force of its victim's resistance, without attracting the same backfire with which the sword, the chain, and the despot have been toppled. Money is so effective because it is necessary and unavoidable. Money functions as societal clay. It constitutes the bolts that hold together nations and states.

On the contrary, money may be regarded as a serious candidate for the most ingenious invention ever. It comprises the idea of trust-based value associated with a carrier that has no intrinsic utility – only "by agreement" it rises to become a medium for trade and wealth accumulation. Money communicates, money binds, money facilitates, and it is the same money that is being turned into a powerful and universal weapon to dangle over all of us.

All that power is hinged on the attribute of universality. Since its inception, money functioned as a storage mechanism for value, for desirability – universal desirability. Whatever your underlying wishes were, money helped. Money facilitates noble causes and evil causes alike. Whether your desires were ordinary or deviant, legal or otherwise, money, universally, is something you want more of. Money moves people to work, sweat, and exert themselves for you. Money moves people to flatter you, offer and extend friendship and love (sincerely or otherwise). Money works regardless of where it came from, independent of what means were used to accumulate it, uninfluenced by any better use thereto. Money has no smell, no history, and no unavoidable moral constraints: if you are in possession of $100, you can readily buy anything that is priced for $100, no questions asked.

MONEY: THE GREAT INVENTION

There is nothing in nature that we all ever want more of, and we all can readily give to each other. That something will have to be unambiguous and measurable. It is safe to say that we all treasure happiness, but we cannot pass two pints of happiness powder from one to the other, can we? Longevity is another viable candidate for universal desire, alas we cannot hand over extra 10 years of longevity. Similarly, for health – who wants to be sick? Only that we cannot transfer a pound of health even to a loved one. Items that can be unambiguous, well measured, and universally desired are not there. Let's consider oxygen – universally needed for all breathing creatures, no doubt about it. And it can be measured as to exact quantity and can be clearly given from Alice to Bob. Only that once we have enough oxygen to fill our lungs, we need no more. Few of us are obsessed about accumulating oxygen tanks in our basement. Same for food, universally consumed, but, like oxygen, our desirability for it trails off from a given point. Most of the things we covet are nonuniversal. Alice may want a nice necklace, but Bob desires a workbench. Neither Alice nor Bob will be happy receiving the other's desire. It may be surprising, but so it is, there is nothing that we all desire, regardless of our particular station in life, age, race, culture, religion, gender, wealth, and that can be readily transferred from one to the other and that we are absolutely certain that whomever we pass that valuable to, will be receptive to it. Nature does not meet our need, so we had to invent it ourselves. And we did. We call it *money*.[1]

The standard textbook definition of money is medium of exchange, a unit of accounting, and a store of value. Very true, but in a deeper sense money is a humanly invented entity that reflects our unity as a society in as much as it is both universally desired and readily passed around among members of our society. Money galvanizes a bunch of separate individuals into a collaborative community. Money is how we motivate, influence, and, yes, manipulate each other.

Exactly because money is so readily transferrable, there is never a rational reason to reject untethered money – money with no restrictions of use. A challenger will claim: some people hold on to some spiritual beliefs that demonize money. Indeed so only that most of those who think so, still desire money, claiming necessity, in this corrupt world of ours. And for the very few who return earned money away: if money is no good, why return it to the payer to whom it would continue to do harm, take it as payment, then destroy it, it's yours, you can burn it, if you wish! Generally, as long as someone around us does not have all the money he or she could use for good purpose, it makes no sense to refuse an offer of earned money (pass it to the needy, if you like).

It is a simple and powerful realization: this mysterious entity that we invented, created, and socially agreed upon, and which we call money, is the one and only entity that is universally desired, measurable, and readily passed around. And as such, it is a prime societal enabler.

MONEY IS POWER

If you were projecting violence, you could have taken from people their possessions and could have forced them to act according to your will. That is exactly what money does – it enables you to take possession of everything that is for sale (few things are not), and it allows you to move people to work for you. And as all rational people desire money, all rational people may be made to do what you want them to do, provided you have enough money to dispense with. The genius of money – as compared to the despot who projects violence – is that money exercises power without raising its subjects to mutiny. This is because, unlike violence that clearly works against its victim's will, money maintains the impression that all is free exchange, free will, and on equal footing. In reality though, the majority of people on earth suppress their free will and act and do to satisfy the will of the one who pays them. The other means for money to be such an accommodated power projector is via the very clever idea of self-reference: Alice makes Bob do what she wants him to do, by paying him money, which,

---

1. What people used for money: wampum: beads made from shells, American Indians; cowries: uniquely shaped colorful shells, India; whales' teeth: used by the Fijians; tobacco: early American colonists; large stone disks: on the pacific island of Yap; cigarettes: World War II; liquor: World War II; cattle: ancient farms communities everywhere; wheat and barley: Babylon; and more: tea, fish, hooks, arrowheads, raw metal, baskets, knives, forks, spoons, and farm tools.

in turn, Bob can use to force Carla to do what he wants *her* to do. And Carla accepts her fate because with the money she receives from Bob, she gets David to follow her command. We all participate in this transactional dance, so we are not inclined to complain, but rather wish to have more of this thing called money, so we can play king or queen more and longer.

Designating money as power does not by itself imply a moral value. The power of money can be used for good, or it can be used for evil. In reality, it is being used for both.

The power associated with money is inherently social: it is power over other people. Moreover, if money is forcibly kept in strictly equal distribution, then it loses its power because Alice then cannot induce Bob to comply with her will, by paying him, as Bob will have to let go of any extra money he accumulates. On the other extreme, if Alice and a few others grab hold of all, or most of the money in circulation, then the other people in her society will have to come up with a different currency to do business among themselves, and Alice's currency will lose its broad societal value. So the power of money comes to an impactful social expression when it is distributed in some way between these two extremes. And society should rightfully ask: what is the distribution of money that will be most beneficial for us as a whole? Namely, not for Alice and Bob as individuals, but for the community in a scoping view.

Society progresses when talented individuals are able to use the power of money (1) to support their living needs, and (2) to invest in their innovation, and exercise their creative initiatives. The first use of money allows the social innovator the time to innovate by being able to have food without being a farmer, and by wearing shoes without being a cobbler. The second use allows him, or her, to tinker, experiment, try, retry, and eventually succeed in gifting society the gift of his, or her, genius. Society will conclude then that such individuals should be given the money they need to succeed.

Now, if all of us would have been tagged with a notice that says how much money we need, and what exactly will be our contribution to society for that investment, then it would have been a dry mathematical challenge to allocate money power to the members of society so that society benefits the most. Alas, no such tags exist. We look at individuals and we have to guess what good they would do to society if given a certain amount of money. And similarly with the moral aspect, society may wish to honor military veterans, retirees, and victims of all sorts, who may have contributed to society for decades, or otherwise are deserving, and the question is: how much will be morally satisfactory to so allocate, without choking societal progress for the generation ahead?

Over the years, two major schools of thoughts have developed to address this challenge of optimal distribution of societal money power. One such economical philosophy, called capitalism, says, let society practice mutual trade. Some will grow rich, others will lose their shirt. Those who became rich via such trade, are obviously the talented ones, and hence, society should keep these nouveau riche attached to their wealth, trusting that they will do the most good with it in the next round. The other economic philosophy, called socialism, says that becoming rich is a matter of luck, probability, and happenstance, and too often, an unfair advantage – no proof of special talent. Hence, the bulk of social power should be siphoned away from the few at the top to give the many at the bottom a second chance to prove themselves. They argue that money corrupts, and much money corrupts more. Hence, it is a good idea not to let any one individual accumulate too much of this corrupting elixir. People with money have a built-in interest to freeze society where it stands, because in the current configuration they are on top. And the more money the rich have, the less money is available to the rest of society – a population with no less probability to include future contributors to the general good. "Perhaps so" answer the capitalists, but corruption and misallocation of resources is equally likely to afflict the particular bureaucrat that society entrusts with the squeezed taxations. Such a custodian of money power is also likely to abuse that power. Even more so, they argue, as she did not earn the budget she is in charge of. These clean-cut principles become very messy in reality. No one would argue that society ought to have stopped Bill Gates after he became rich developing the PC operating system DOS. Choking taxation would have prevented Mr Gates from developing Windows. However, few would disagree today that to smash AT&T (Ma Bell), to its corporate pieces (Baby Bells), allowed for breathtaking creativity in the field of communication. In real political fights, these two schools of thoughts come down to one says: reduce taxes (however low they may be), let the rich hold on to more of their spoils, and lift society in their wake, whereas the other says: tax the rich more than they are being taxed today (whatever it is), and give the tax spoils to thoughtful government bureaucrats to wisely use this power to lift up the less-fortunate ones.

In one way, the wealthy private citizens (owners) and the budget-wealthy government bureaucrats (custodians) are highly similar. They both loathe visibility and transparency. Anyone who has money to dispense with, is desirous of secrecy as to how much money goes where and for what reason. The greater the secrecy, the greater the power. The more opaque the payment process, the broader the latitude to the one who controls the funds.

Let's consider an extreme case: a government bureaucrat in charge of billions of dollars finds himself shackled by a detailed procedure that guides the allocation of these billions. There is nothing left for the bureaucrat's discretion, it is all spelled out and specified. Would this bureaucrat be considered powerful? Not really. Come to think about it, this bureaucrat will be readily replaceable by a computer program.

Say more, if the ability to pay money is the expression of modern nonviolent social power, then the power wielders would naturally aspire to total freedom to use their money as they see fit, but societal interest is to insure, at the very least, that visibility and transparency will reign. Much as improvement in any field or endeavor hinges first on the ability to *measure* how good the situation is right now, and whether it improves or otherwise, so it is with our attempt to insure improvement of money allocation in society: one first needs maximum visibility as to what use was given to money today. Visibility of payment dynamics is a foundation for a scientific approach to the challenge of societal distribution of money power.

Throughout all the expressions of money thus far, the desire for secrecy prevailed. Money changed hands under the table, behind closed doors, and via unresolved thefts and coercions, and robberies. The remarkable prospect today is to express money in a digital tethered form to greatly enhance the visibility of its flow patterns – if society so desires, while switching off this view and establishing controlled anonymity, to insure a good measure of privacy for the trading community.

MONEY: MAN-MADE MYSTERY

The structure of the cosmos, the assembly of life, and subatomic particles are all mysteries we have encountered in our life-long introductory journey into reality. By contrast, money is man-made, easily understood at par value, yet it is no less mysterious, no less multifaceted, and perhaps even no less powerful, no less essential, and no less promising than the opening list.

Money is the most tangible of things, and the most abstract of things; money is the most practical issue, and the most airy topic; money is the most exact metric of transactional value, and the most equivocal attribute of personal value. Money looks completely different when it is in one's pocket than when it is a topic of pondering and analysis. Money evokes different reaction when it is something you owe or something you earned. Money is a wished-for blessing – notice how many well-wishing cards invoke wealth and how many silent prayers beg for more of it. Money is a curse – just read the histories of war, or follow stories of hatred, jealousy, greed, and belligerency throughout history. Money arose as a practical solution to a paramount societal problem, alas, it side-evolved into a tool of tyranny, a device for social engineering, a disguised weapon, and soon, as this book envisions, money will be rendered by technology into the key to the magic garden of global prosperity.

Money deserves our attention: nobody is impartial to it. It's a universal desire to have more money, to have less debt. So deeply are we involved in earning it, grabbing it, hoarding it, storing, safekeeping, and hiding it that we hardly take a bird's view of the same. If we allow ourselves a momentary rise to bird's heights, peering into the future of money, we may see a bright prospect on account of two factors: the Internet and the invention of digital currency. Combined, the two allow for money to be all that it was meant to be – the facilitator of societal growth and prosperity. Society grows when its members are well motivated to contribute their best, and money is, by its very essence, a universal motivator. Indeed money is impactful. Well handled it will dramatically impact our society for the better; ill handled it would impede, hurt, harm, and even disintegrate our society into its abandon.

Isn't it a trifle too colorful, aren't these words contaminated by hype? People are motivated by their conviction, idealism, and morality; it's not all about money, money, and money. Well, let us describe how a moneyless society looks like, a thought experiment, as Einstein was fond of saying. Suppose that all of a sudden all electronic accounts in the world show 000000, and all the coins and the bills disappear in an instant. We still have our homes, our cars, our packed pantries, and all our clothes; we simply don't have the comfort of visible big numbers in the web page entitled "our account." How would life proceed? As no employee can be paid, no one will show up for work. No, you said, people are patriotic and mindful; they will show up to work, hoping for a solution to be found. Alas, the stores will not be opened, and will conduct no business because nobody has money to pay for anything. People will find themselves wanting the essentials of life. In a very short time, riots will erupt as people march on stores and supply centers to get milk, eggs, shoes, and toilet paper. But these supply centers will soon be empty because the suppliers will stop manufacturing their products as their workers will not show up, and their customers can't pay them. Self-reliance gangs will form and replace the civil order. One would conjecture that before society collapses, a new form of currency would be devised. The dollar is dead, long live the new money: be it gold, medicine, guns, or bullets; people will desperately search for a substance that is universally desired, and hence transactable, and also a good way to store value and manage books. This horror scenario describes the unfolding of a surprise event wherein money records disappear. When the accounts, the bills, and the coins disappear, they don't destroy anything "real"; no beams are removed from buildings or bridges, no fertile land is washed away, and no tsunami is sweeping houses out to sea; there remains enough oxygen to breathe, same amount of drinking water, no change in the roads, or in the amount of gas ready to be distilled in the refineries. Nothing "real" has changed, and yet, society comes to a shrieking halt.

This scenario highlights the role of money as a societal mover and motivator. Money keeps people busy, active, ambitious, and productive. People exploit their talent and energy to build, construct, and assemble entities that are worth paying for and that would earn them money. These abstract figures marked on computer files, these worth-nothing paper bills, and the worth-little coins flow about in society and their flow keeps society moving, humming, growing, innovating, and prospering!

This scenario also highlights the vaporware nature of money – no physical, tangible entity disappeared when the accounts were zeroed out. As paper and coins amount to about 11% of the circulating currency, they could not sustain a payment regimen on their own. Say then that even if only the computerized numbers had disappeared, the paralysis described earlier would have happened much the same. It is frightening to think that some massive disruption of the electromagnetic signs on chips and on data storage devices would trigger a global catastrophe with chain reaction consequences.

And if so, could not the simple resurrection of numbers on accounts serve as a cure, even if the original numbers are forgotten, and new numbers are selected?

Or what if the government will react to such a money wipeout with a decreed distribution of 1000 new currency units to every citizen in the country? Well, this would work. People will have an initial sum to pay and new currency to get paid with. Society will be primed up. Of course, prices will have to be adjusted to allow commerce to start-up, and build up, and we might all readily expect that those who accumulated money before the wipeout will be the ones to get rich in this new currency paradigm. Over time, the evolving gradient of money will likely resemble the old gradient, and the same for the economy in the new paradigm, it will trend to track the economy in the old paradigm. Alas, those who simply inherited a lot of money from their ancestors, however, themselves lacking the skills to make money, will be the losers from this exercise because they would lose their fortune and be unequipped with the skills to reaccumulate it.

Come to think about it, this specter of a new currency replacing the established national currencies engenders a real fear in the powers that be. They are fully aware of the fact that dollars, euros, and yen remain and stay functional because … they are expected to remain and stay functional. And they know that there is no magic to the dollar bill, or the euro coin, it simply reigns, and its reign may be wrestled away from it by any storming newcomer currency. And that is why every country is very serious with respect to banks, financial institutions, and other entities that may sneak into society with a newly minted currency.

There were several attempts in the United States to trade with specialty dollars – and the federal government came down on them like a ton of bricks. Fortunately, something has changed. Technology is running amok, driven by a complexity of market forces. A barrage of new scientific gadgets is flooding our streets; distances have been shrunk, this whole planet has become a single web. What is happening in one end of the globe is seen, felt, and reported in all other ends. Seven billion people face each other as virtual neighbors, and when so, they interact, transact, pay and get paid, store value, bank, extend credit, mitigate risk, and, soon enough, build a financial platform and a digital currency to make this happen. There is no force in the world that can prevent it. That is the difference today. Until now, the power of the fiat currencies and the governments who mint and manage them was strong enough to suppress competition and insure durable dominance. No longer. Much as we have seen dictators and tyrannies around the world thrown out of power, or being reformed by the surprise force of the social tsunami unleashed by the Internet (social media), so the old time money lords, who will fail to adapt, will eventually lose their hold on how people pay, get paid, move, get moved, and innovate and prosper. Society should identify in its midst the new cadre of leaders that will have the clear view of this amazing paradigm shift, and lead with a steady hand, on a global scale. Technology offers the tools for ill or for thrill, and it is up to us to be smart, strong, and mindful to put these tools into good use.

This book describes the imminent reality wherein new forms of money not only come to the fore and create an unprecedented opportunity for innovation and prosperity, but also are subject to clever and abusive exploitation by the hidden powers that used today's and yesterday's money platform to stay in power, and castle-up their position at the top. This small book was written to serve as a precursor to a comprehensive roadmap for money in the first decades of the twenty-first century. It is no more than a first glance at the road to be taken (hopefully) or to be shunned (regrettably).

MONEY: MIRAGE

Alice opens a checking account with her bank, and deposits $1000 in it. Alice now walks around with her checkbook, feeling empowered; she can pay anyone any sum up to $1000, just like before, when she held the $1000 in banknotes. The bank, on its part, will normally keep, say, $100 to respond to a sudden demand, and loan the other $900 to Bob. What happened? Before the money was deposited only Alice had it, and was empowered by it. But now Alice is still empowered, she can draw a check for up to $1000, at any moment, to whomever! But the bank also behaves as the owner of the same money. And what about Bob? He now controls $900 of that original $1000. What happened, how did the money double and triple itself? Furthermore, Bob will probably deposit his $900 loan (minus some immediate expenses) in his bank, which will keep, say, $100 for reserve and loan $750 to Carla. More and more people behave and feel like they have money, which amounts to a mirage: money pops up as an illusory vision. *How exactly does this work?*

Millions of Americans write a check for $20,000 and buy a house worth $250,000, fully registered in their name. Alas, the bank that paid the difference to the seller owns something called a "*deed of trust*" to the same house, and is likely to sell this deed as the owner of the property. So who actually owns the house, the buyer, or the lender? How can the same piece of property be in possession of two different claimants?

A man pays $500 to an insurance company and buys insurance for a quarter of million dollars for his home. This mystery is a bit more familiar, and less mysterious, but its root is the same as the above: probabilities. The insurance company relies on historic data to compute the chances for someone losing his home, and by selling insurance to many customers, its expectation for profit are well anchored on rigorous math. With the house, the ownership question reminds one of the famous "Schrödinger Cat," the quantum mechanical premise that says that reality is undetermined until it is actually observed. When the house deal is done, it is not clear whether the deed of trust will be activated and the bank ends up the owner, or whether the monthly payments will be made in order, and the buyer will become the *de facto* owner. The bank has good statistics about payment defaults and gauges its risk by setting up the interest rate. In the case of Alice deposit, the bank knows how frequently depositors write checks and for which sums, so the bank can adjust its reserve to meet these needs.

What if these underlying probabilities surprise us and go haywire? In that case, the defense that relies on them is shattered: a strong hurricane destroying thousands of homes might bring the insurance company to its knees. An economic depression prevents homeowners from making their mortgage payments – and the lender ends up owning neighborhoods. If some rumor creates a run on the bank, the bank will exhaust its reserves, and collapse – unless some safety net is provided, as we shall see ahead. But for perspective, let's remember that our entire civil order is based on the science of probabilities: if for some reasons lots of houses catch fire, there will not be enough firefighters. If an epidemic bursts, there will be shortage of healthcare personnel. If too many people hit the same road at the same time, there will be a traffic jam.

Although the science and math of probabilities is rock solid, and properly used, it supports banks, insurance companies, and many other major institutions reflecting modern life, it too often happens that the math is misapplied, with disasters to follow. It's not a matter of fraud, just incompetence. To illustrate the propensity for mistakes, consider the case of the popular prize game wherein a contester was asked to choose among three doors, knowing that one of the three doors opens into a garage where a brand new shining Ferrari is waiting to be picked up. With the audience over national TV biting its proverbial nails, the contester trembles and points to one of the doors. The master of ceremony is about to open that door, but stops, and in a surprise move, opens another door – it shows an empty garage. The MC then turns to the contester: "I am prepared to allow you to switch your choice from the door you selected to the other door that is still closed. Would you switch?" In reality, most contesters would stick with their original choice, believing, probably, that some all-knowing spirit guided their original choice, and therefore they should remain faithful to their intuition. Later interviewed, contesters argue that they figured out that the chance for the Ferrari to be behind either door is the same (50%), so it made no sense to switch. The case became a national debate, with some highly respected mathematicians supporting the 50:50 conclusion. But it is wrong, the rational choice is to switch – it doubles the chances to win the luxury car. We will not digress into the math here, and refocus on our point: probability math is prone to drastic mistakes. When used in high-stake finance, such mistakes will rock the markets.

MONEY: MIRAGE FRAUD

The mirage of money multiplication also happens through mechanisms that do not have probability as an anchor, but are clear fraud, usually well hidden. Let's focus on three very common broad categories of fraud: (1) the short-range fraud, (2) reconciliation fraud, and (3) confusion fraud.

Short Range

The idea here is that an enticing argument appears valid, if applied sparingly, and if applied to its full measure, it fails. The most common example is known as "Ponzi Scheme." Here is a simple example. Alice proposes to Bob to join in the following "game." "I received an ordered list of five people." Alice says. "I send $1.00 to the person at the head of the list, then I erased him from the list, and added my name, Alice, at the bottom of the list. Now I am looking for five people to pass this list to. Should you agree to play, Bob, you should do what I did: send $1.00 to the person at the head of the list, erase his name from the list, and add yours, Bob, at the bottom. You see, Bob," Alice argues, "all that you pay is one single lousy dollar, and then you enlist five people to join the game. Now, mathematically, it is obvious that if the game continues, and the five people you recruited, recruit five others in their circles, and these new recruits keep the same simple procedure, then you will receive a sum total of $3125 (for an investment of $1.00!). How can you turn me down, Bob? The logic is impeccable, the return on your investment is skyrocketing, the risk is one lousy dollar!" Now, what is wrong with this picture? Well, it is the *short-range fraud category*: it works only if you look at a short range from the first person that started it. Why? Because the scheme works by constantly signing up more and more payers. At some point, there would not be enough people in the world to keep the scheme going. For early joiners, the scheme is indeed very profitable. The money comes from the very many at the tail end, and this majority at the end of the game feed the early adopters.

Reconciliation

If Alice pays Bob one quarter, then at any given moment the coin is either still in Alice's possession, or already in Bob's hands. It cannot be held by both at the very same time. This simple certainty, regrettably, has been lost with the abstraction of money into accounting systems. When Alice pays Bob through her bank account, or via her payment card, etc., she does not toss over a coin to Bob; she, instead, agrees on matching actions. Bob will increment the number that represents the money in his disposal (normally written in his account on the clouds), and Alice will decrement her account by the same amount. When both Alice and Bob have concluded their actions, the payment is considered done. This abstraction of the old plain toss-over of a coin introduces the issue of reconciliation: suppose Bob is faster than Alice and increments his account before she decrements hers. In that case, for a certain period of time, we have the "mirage" of doubling the money – the same quarter appears both on Alice's books and on Bob's books. Come to think about it, each time Alice cuts a check and hands it over to Bob, she puts the face value of the check in limbo for the period of time between handing over the check and cashing the same. As a result, when banks and large financial transactions institutions "freeze check" their accounts, they detect myriad of inconsistencies that need to be reconciled. This reconciliation task is a major burden for banks. It is also a fertile ground for conmen, fraudsters, and thieves, which are rich on imagination. Oddly enough digital money automatically resolves this problem, because it operates like physical coins and banknotes – a digital coin, like a regular coin, is either in Alice's possession or in Bob's hands – no reconciliation needed.

To further emphasize the mirage enigma of money, let us come back to physical cash. Ten banks in the state claim to the bank examiner that they have $1 million in their reserve, at any moment. Alas, in reality, the 10 banks can pull together only $1 million, namely, they are $9 million short. The examiner does not take the bank's word, and launches spot checks to verify their declaration. Now suppose that the banks managed to lay hand on the examiner's visit schedule, and they know ahead of time which bank would be examined when. In that case, the banks in cahoots would pass the million bucks to the bank about to be visited. The examiner, over time, would find that every bank has the claimed $1 million reserve, and the banking system is safe. This case demonstrates how a small piece of crucial intelligence may turn a financial picture upside down.

Confusion

The abstraction of money and payment leading to the issue of reconciliation will mushroom further into persistent vagueness and confusion – a smoke screen hiding theft, fraud, and abuse on a very large scale. This is why accountants must be trustworthy because it is their art of classification, summation, and reconciliation that can be wielded to create massive fraud and catastrophic deceptions. Enron, Bernard Madoff, The Lehman Brothers, are notorious examples. A popular joke talks about a mathematician, an engineer, and an accountant who were all asked how much is 2×2. The mathematician said 2^2, the engineer said the answer is larger than 3.9999 and smaller than 4.0001, and the accountant, on his part, pulled the inquirer to the side, and whispered in his ears: "How much would you like it to be?" The confusion of money and payment is further illustrated by the following two stories: (1) the coffee shop visitor – a man walked into a coffee shop and ordered an apple pie. When he was served, he decided to change his mind, shoved the pie back, and asked for a cheesecake. He enjoyed the cake and walked away. The man behind the counter yelled at him: "What about paying?" "Paying for what?" the visitor asked.

"For the cheesecake!"

"I gave you an apple pie for it, remember?"

"Ok, so pay for the apple pie!"

"Why should I pay for an apple pie I did not eat?"

This trick behind this simple story is routinely used in settlement discussions, and in court room dramas, confusing even the best and the brightest.

(2) The basketball – Peter, Paul, and Mary decided to buy a basketball together. They went to a high-class sport goods store and spotted a nice ball. The price tag on the ball was $30.00. So Peter, Paul, and Mary contributed $10 each, and went out with the ball. A minute later, the shop clerk is catching up with them, apologizing for overlooking the fact that the ball was on sale, and its cost today was only $25.00. The clerk then gives the three buyers a bundle of five $1 bills. Peter, Paul, and Mary were impressed with the display of honesty, so they each took a $1 bill back, and the remaining two bucks they returned to the clerk as a token of their appreciation. Walking onward, Mary raises the following

question: we have originally paid $10.00 each, and we each got $1 back, so we each paid $9.00 for the ball, or $27.00 in sum, plus the $2 we gave the clerk, it comes to $29, but we have paid $30 to begin with – where is the missing dollar? A careful thought will resolve this mystery quite quickly, but it too illustrates the power of accounting confusion and its impact on money flow.

SELF-ANCHORED MONEY

In 1971, President Nixon took a bold step. He self-anchored the US dollar. Nixon severed the former anchor, gold, and replaced it with the tautology: *the dollar is a dollar. If you bring a dollar to the bank, you get a dollar in return.* It was a daring gamble to count on trade inertia. The street, by and large, ignored this historic statement, and prices for a while remained the same.

Self-anchored digital money proponents point to Nixon when arguing the integrity of their currency. It does not wash. President Nixon represented the US government. He had the power to fix prices by decree (and he did), outlaw the use of nondollar currencies (as president Roosevelt did with respect to gold), and insist on getting paid, and paying off in US dollars. Nixon could tax America "to death," and he was the leader of the most potent economic powerhouse in history. No digital currency has anything of the sort.

Self-anchored digital currencies are mathematical creatures. Mathematics is undoubtedly one of the foundational pillars of civilization, but at the same time, it is the avenue of imagination, and the manufacturer of dreams, illusions, and mind-boggling entities. Math deals with something called imaginary numbers – the square root of -1. Such a number does not exist, so math gives birth to it, by decree, and does wonders with this invention of an imaginary creation. Math concludes that the set of natural numbers 1, 2, 3, ... while uncapped, inexhaustible (infinite), is still a smaller set than the number of dots on a line. Mathematicians acknowledge that this premise is inconsistent with commonsense, but for a mathematician, whenever commonsense and mathematical proof disagree, the proof prevails. The paradox inherent in the sentence "This statement is a lie" (which can't be neither a true statement nor a false one) is resolved through tortured logic that also quashes commonsense. Even the basic premise that logical arguments can be applied in a series to conclude a clear and true statement has been shattered by Kurt Godel (1931), who proved that consistent application of logical reasoning results in a statement that is either unclear or inconsistent with the statements leading to it. The great mathematician and logician Bertrand Russell said "Mathematics may be defined as the subject in which we never know what we are talking about, nor whether what we are saying is true." G. H. Hardy observed that in mathematics, truth plays odd pranks more than in any other subject. Mathematics works by building inferential consistency among a set of premises. As long as there exists mutual consistency, it does not matter if the outside world regards it as nonsense. That observation prompted Russell's description of math. And this applies very well to self-contained definition of money and payment. As long as the entities, the rules, and the algorithms are mutually consistent, it works – for those who live in that mathematical world. Indeed, bitcoin traders can accumulate money, pass money, and trade with money – regardless of anything that happens outside. In that respect, bitcoin is like the game of Monopoly. Both are games where money is well defined, and where it is used when the game is played. Any link between that internal money and a more generally accepted money simply reflects the attraction of the game.

Suppose that some celebrities come together to play Monopoly on TV. They play in installments, and the crowds go wild. The players are ambitious so player Alice proposes to Bob to buy from him some of his Monopoly money to improve her standing in the game. In fact, Alice is so interested in the game that she offers US $10 for one Monopoly dollar. Carla realizing that her competitive position relative to Alice has now deteriorated, will approach Bob, offering him US $20 for $1 Monopoly. Very quickly, the trade between Monopoly money and US dollar heats up, the price goes through the roof ... But is there any doubt that sooner or later interest in the game will wane, and Monopoly dollars will lose their value versus "real dollars?" Bitcoin in the present form (2015) is the same: a game that triggered universal interest, generating an ad-hoc price for its currency. Like in a Ponzi scheme, the early adopters of bitcoin scored big. The currency is kept afloat by its strong anonymity feature that attracts the dark siders of humanity, but its infirmity is as intrinsic as Monopoly money. There is absolutely no objective rational for any particular exchange value between a Monopoly dollar and a US dollar, or between a bitcoin and a US dollar. The early price of bitcoin, 9 pennies, makes as much economic sense as the highest price ever $1200.

Here is a scenario to sharpen the point. Let us, for the sake of argument, agree with the bitcoin traders that the bitcoin protocol is perfect, or nearly so. There is no better way to do money than bitcoin. Bitcoin price history shows that the early adopters made a "killing" – their rate of return was astronomical. The latecomers see little uptake, even some down slopes. They would be tempted then to launch a bitcoin 2 – a currency that operates exactly as bitcoin 1 – a copy of the protocol, with one distinction: it is called bitcoin 2, and it trades only in bitcoin 2 coins. Bitcoin 1 (the original bitcoin) is not recognized in the boundaries of bitcoin 2. Much like bitcoin 1, bitcoin 2 will start very low. Bitcoin 2 will be worth 1 penny to start with. Trading right along bitcoin 1, more and more traders in the old bitcoin will reason that hopping onto the new bitcoin is smart, as its price can only go one way – up. And as the protocol of bitcoin 2 is the same as the protocol of bitcoin 1, it will not hold water to deride the competing currency and argue that it is not as robust, tight, secure, convenient, or, otherwise, valuable as the old bitcoin. It is the very same protocol, very same advantages, and very same disadvantages. No difference, except the price. So if Alice likes bitcoin 1, she would equally like bitcoin 2; not equally – more, because the price is expected to go up. Following this situation onward, one would conclude that the price of bitcoin 1 will drop as traders sell their bitcoin

1 for some fiat currency, dollar, euro, etc., and then use this fiat currency to buy bitcoin 2. The latter will soar. This counter trends will continue until the price of the two equal protocol bitcoins will be one and the same. But would that price be stable? No way. Someone will reapply the very same protocol to a new currency, bitcoin 3, and its price will soar at the expense of the falling prices of bitcoin 1 and bitcoin 2. This exercise of protocol duplication cannot be repeated with, say, dollars or euros because these currencies represent their respective economies. Also, bitcoin proponents argue that bitcoin is like gold, the number of bitcoins is capped at 21 million units, which makes it a modern twin to the trusted gold basis. Quite an outreach, one would have to admit. It is clearly impossible to launch a gold-2 and gold-3 ... And as for the limit, the launch of bitcoin 2 instantly doubled the limit to 42 million coins.

Self-anchored mathematical, game money cannot realistically hope for a stable exchange rate with money that is backed by human commodities; more than a million dollar prize, one receives in her dreams, can be cashed in the local bank, after she wakes up.

MONEY ON BEHALF OF THE PEOPLE (CENTRAL BANKS)

And because money is mysterious, and money is power, and money is universal, the forces applied over it are not limited to trade, business, and commerce. Crime, abuse, violence, and wonton taxation are all pushing and pulling money and skewing its distribution. Some of these forces are dark and evil; some are irresponsible and irrational. As civilization matured into well-organized states, societies asserted their inalienable power and established a political mechanism to hand over the right to govern, to elected representatives, custodians of the recognized power of the people. This maturity established the army, the police, the welfare state, all the organs of tranquil, and productive life. Managing currency became front and center. It was usually a department of treasury that took that initiative. The problem with that was that the politics of the moment influenced monetary actions that should be based and aimed at long-term goals. The instability leading to World War I moved the US Congress to establish the US Federal Reserve System. The system serves as the nation's central bank. It was created by The Federal Reserve Act, on December 23, 1913. The System consists of a seven-member Board of Governors with headquarters in Washington, DC, and 12 Reserve Banks located in major cities throughout the United States. The seven members of the Board of Governors are appointed by the President and confirmed by the Senate to serve 14-year terms of office. Members may serve only one full term, but a member who has been appointed to complete an unexpired term may be reappointed to a full term. The President designates, and the Senate confirms, two members of the Board to be Chairman and Vice Chairman, for 4-year terms. Only one member of the Board may be selected from any one of the 12 Federal Reserve districts. In making appointments, the President is directed by law to select a "fair representation of the financial, agricultural, industrial, and commercial interests and geographical divisions of the country." These aspects of selection are intended to ensure representation of regional interests and the interests of various sectors of the public.

The establishing act provides for latitude and independence. The Federal Reserve System is autonomous in its decisions – there is neither a need for a Congressional vote, nor a presidential directive. Yet, what the Congress gives, the Congress can take away. Also, the independent judicial system is ready to intervene and rule on any emerging dispute regarding the authority or actions of the Federal Reserve. Hence, the popular myth propagated by some bitcoin proponents that the Central Bank is run by stuck-up arrogant imperials who answer to nobody, is simply not true. The people through their representatives can impact, influence, modify, and even "kill" the Federal Reserve, which is not the case with respect to the shadowy crew that runs, modifies, and regulates the bitcoin trading protocol. It is fitting to also remember that Congress, like parliaments elsewhere, still maintains the strings to the spending purse, and levy taxes that siphon away cash from the people. Noted economists like Robert Rubin, a former US secretary of the Treasury, warned about the moral hazard of politicians shaking off monetary responsibility, pointing a finger at the central bank. It is very disturbing to contemplate a scenario wherein the executive branch of government acts in a contradictory way toward the steps taken by the central bank. It should be noted that it was the Obama US Treasury that applied enormous pressures on international banks trading in the United States, to comply with US Anti Money Laundering laws, not the Federal Reserve.

Another distinction between Congress and the Federal Reserve is that the former is comprised of politicians for whom the prime competence is the skill to get elected, and reelected, whereas the Federal Reserve is run by a hierarchy of complementing professionals enjoying long-term appointments.

The Congress has launched the Federal Reserve with a high-level mandate to help secure low unemployment, keep prices stable, and arrest interest rate at acceptable low rates. The main tools to achieve these goals are open-market operations in government securities, lending via its discount window, and setting reserve requirements on bank deposits.

The nature of the Federal Reserve is indirect control, as opposed to command control. The Federal Reserve determines the prime interest rate, which instantly affects the street rates, but the intended result may be different from the actual one. The Federal Reserve can flood the market with fiat money or restrict money flow, but again, the purpose of that action may be subverted on account of the complexity and uncertainty of how millions of people will react to these impositions.

Some are looking at the 100-year history of the Federal Reserve and conclude that the Federal Reserve is populated with magicians endowed with profound understanding of the market. The "few" crises is a shadow of what could have happened in a country the size of the United States, where individual freedom is so pervasive and anyone can so easily start a company, engage in business, buy, sell, and constantly find new ways to make money, and risk his or other people treasures. Experts on the opposite side point to the Great Depression of 1929 and the subsequent poor years, as well as the 2008 world crisis, as an indication that the Federal Reserve does not have a good grip on the complexity of their task.

The reality is that the complexity of societal behavior defies sound and credible modeling. Nobel Prize laureates and other academics persist in offering explanations and mathematical modeling to guide the Federal Reserve, as well as the stock market, foreign exchange, etc., but nothing so far has proven itself for the long run.

It may be a sobering digression to mention here the story of long-term capital management (LTCM). Star-quality mathematicians built a risk model they used to guide investment. They merged with market mavens, and offered their services to rich and ambitious investors. For a while, their results outperformed the market with a huge edge. But in 1998, one fundamental risk assessment in the model gave in and the profit edifice came crashing down. LTCM fell prey to a common miscalculation: misappraisal of the probability of a rare, harmful event. Model builders imagine a few such events, calculate their accumulated probability, and show that it is comfortably low. Alas, some rare events have never happened before, so model builders may not be aware of them, and although the probability of each such hidden event may be very low, the cumulative probability for any of them to take place is quite unsettling. Mathematicians and scientists are used to a certain measure of computational errors, and to correct them the next time around. Only that global finance is not an experiment with mice; it defines the fortunes and agonies of millions of people. The LTCM principles were endowed Nobel prize in economics (before the collapse, of course), highlighting the dangerous trend to overtrust mathematical exercises. Quite a lesson for today, as we contemplate the bitcoin assertion that they have spotted an algorithm that will generate a new better currency for humanity.

The *Wall Street Journal* cast notorious stock pickers against a random dart thrown at the big board. For any short range of time, some experts shone bright, but over the longer run, the random dart outperformed the self-acclaimed "sofisticados." Similarly, the Federal Reserve is using some heavy-duty analytics and sophisticated indexing, but on top of all, the "geek stuff" rides the intuitive wisdom of the leadership team. They are good, but not perfect. In hindsight, one would argue that the great depression of 1929 and the second great crisis of 2008 could have been prevented, but looking forward, if not this crisis, than another would have hit.

What's more: the "blame game" regarding the still fresh and painful 2008 crisis is raging wild, with books anew proposing theses, antitheses, and syntheses galore. One analysis points to President Clinton desire to help the lower strata of society to become the homeowners class. Political science teaches us that homeowners are more stable, better-rooted people than renters, drifters, and stay-at-mom's-home crowd. Homeowners develop a sense of belonging to their community and are more likely to contribute to them. Homeowners are docile at work, because it would be a catastrophe if they get fired and miss a mortgage payment, so no rebel rousing. And so politicians applied pressure on local banks to relax the security checks and confirm more would-be homeowners. Bankers are beholden to politicians, as they keep the law and the regulatory climate in their favor, and so they yielded. Suddenly a fountain of real-estate buyers popped up, and prices rose. As they did they cemented the argument that it is a good idea to buy a house you cannot afford, but insist on balloon payments so that initially the monthly payment will be affordable. And what about the "balloon time?" Well, don't worry about that, because in a year or two, the value of your house will rise so much that you will sell it with an obscene profit and immediately turn around to buy a much bigger house. An uplifting dynamics developed. And everyone was happy: the buyers who could not afford a home, now had one, and those who lived in modest houses, now lived in mansions. The banks loved the high subprime interest they could charge, and they shunned their increased risk by chopping these assets and repackaging them according to some complex formula that insured low risk by virtue of diversification. The dynamics fed on itself. Profits and economic fortunes favored all. Only a disinterested sober observer would have noted that it is much like a Ponzi scheme that enriches all the early adopters and accelerates up until it hits a wall. The wall came in 2008. In retrospect, the profit motive overwhelmed all caution, and it is likely to happen again in a different form. Our only hope is the cumulative wisdom of the experienced and the thoughtful. The Federal Reserve surely had the power to issue cooling regulations, Congress could have legislated in favor of a better outcome, and the US treasury had a say. Bankers, the real-estate community, etc., could have acted "more responsibly" – could have … And maybe they have done many smart moves that prevented similar crises earlier. It is instructive to think through this crisis and ask oneself, could a mathematical currency devoid of any central bank and unmanaged by any executive or director prevented this crisis? Had the nine-page article by Satoshi Nakamoto captured all the wisdom necessary to keep money and society in a happy marriage? Should we trust cryptography rather than our fellow man? The bitcoin announcement article says "What is needed is an electronic payment system based on cryptographic proof instead of trust."

In 1950, Claude Shannon proposed the idea of a computer chess – an algorithm that would beat human chess masters. His innovative article "Programming a Computer for Playing Chess" was followed by others, and the concept was developed and elaborated on for about 50 years. It was almost half a century later, in 1997, when IBM Deep Blue achieved the milestone of beating the human champion Kasparov (barely). Taking computer chess as a reference to computer money, one would expect that somewhere in the middle of this century, the prevailing currency would be in part built and defined via computer algorithms. The medical analogy comes to mind. Computer diagnostics is still not nearly as refined as human physicians' analysis, but for a patient afflicted with a rare disease, the computer is more likely to suspect it. Future physicians will likely rely on a computer companion, for their intimate decisions, and so will central bankers. We may see a day when the Federal Reserve prints and removes from circulation "cyber dollars" via an elaborate computer system reading millions of data points, second by second. But bitcoin, as it was proposed in 2008, is not it.

As economies evolve and diverge the complexity of money flow increases; there are ever more people wielding larger sums of money to satisfy ever more numerous needs, making ever more decisions as to disposition of their currency. The Internet and the global village will only accelerate this trend. Such a sizzling dynamics can at any moment take a turn for the worse and avalanche into a total monetary collapse. The task of the central bank is to prevent that from happening and, furthermore, keep the money dynamics stable and healthy. The establishment act of the Federal Reserve goes further: the role of the central bank is to keep unemployment down. Some Federal Reserve chairpersons believed they have a mandate to safeguard social justice, and other political goals, which the executive and legislative branches of government fail to carry out, owing perhaps to a political gridlock. To accomplish this tall order, the central bank needs a hefty set of tools. And above all, the bank needs full control over the currency of the people. This basic premise is a simple reason why the unseasoned calls for imminent replacement of fiat currency with mathematical game currency are so naive. Central banks have the power of the states behind them: they can call in legislation, and can summon police and law enforcement agencies. They fight with money, but they also fight with guns, if they have to. It is therefore that every serious scenario for the money of the foreseeable future must somehow include fiat currencies. In Europe, a first of its kind experiment is being conducted. Countries that remain independent and run by their own governments are nonetheless bound by a tight union and have submitted to a unity currency. The advantages are obvious; state-to-state trade is free from the burden of daily oscillating exchange rate. But the underlying result is that central bank duties are pushed up to the European Central Bank, as each member country has no longer the power to manage its own money. Theoretically, the European Central Bank has to balance the interests of all member countries, but in reality, the interests of the more affluent, controlling countries weigh more.

Central banks control the supply of their fiat currency: they "print" more of it or they remove its excess. Central banks dictate interest rates, and control the exposure and risk of the country's financial institutions. The underlying objective of the central bank is to keep the currency stable. Currency is inherently unstable, a casual rise in value may lead to a steep deflation, and a random loss of value may start a collapsing avalanche – all on account of human crowd psychology. The challenge for the central bank is to counter this crowd psychology, and the central bank needs sufficient power to do that. The central bank has to act very accurately, very specifically in terms of monetary actions, and in terms of carving, managing, and controlling a host of financial instruments, but unlike a car mechanic who has to fix your car, and being friendly is a nice extra, central banks must exude trust and inspire faith. It would be very difficult to prevent a rebellious populace from shifting to gold, or to other currencies, should the central bank project an air of confusion, hesitation, and incompetence. The words, the tone, and the off-the-cuff remarks of central bankers have moved the stock and bond markets in big swings.

Stability is the first objective because to the extent that money is unstable, it is no longer money. And stability is essential for the credit market to bloom. Credit is the rocket fuel that sends the economy soaring. But right next to stability comes the objective of exchange value vs. the fiat currencies with which the country has the highest trade activity. Exporters wish the home fiat currency to be weak because then they net more money from their sales abroad. The tourism industry comes right along: a weak currency attracts foreign visitors. At the same time, industries that purchase equipment supplies abroad for a local market are hurting by a low currency: inflationary pressures mount and interest rates rise, suffocating local growth. At any point in time, it is arguable, and experts debate, whether from here it is better to lower or better to jack up the value of the local fiat currency. But one issue is settled: it's never a good idea to swing the value of the currency up and down. It creates uncertainty that suffocates daring business activity.

Much like insurance companies, banks operate on probabilities. Structurally, banks are doomed to collapse when their depositors all decide to withdraw their money. They simply don't have the funds ready because the lion share of it went out as loans – that is how banks make money: the spread between the interest charged for the loans and the interest they pay to their depositors. A fraction of the deposit remains in the bank, ready to honor normal demands for cash. The measure of this fraction reflects the risk undertaken by the bank, risk that is calculated by bankers and economists. Oftentimes banks will take high risks and become victims of a negative rumor that sends depositors to the bank counters, withdrawing their funds – crashing the bank. When this happens, the depositors are left hat in hand, many losing their lives savings. It is therefore that central banks decided to weigh in, impose regulations, and manage risk for ordinary depositors. In the United States, the central bank (the Federal Reserve) issued an insurance program (The Federal Deposit Insurance Corporation, FDIC). Banks pay into it and are helped out by it if their own risk management fails.

The surge of digital money poses a new challenge for the central banks. Digital money is stored in cryptographic vaults, found on PC, tablets, and smartphones. If the interest offered by the bank to its depositors is too low, then the depositors will opt for cryptostorage under their personal control. For banks, the deposits are the raw material they work with. Absent deposits banks collapse. For a central bank, the situation wherein most of the money in the hands of the public is found in bank accounts is convenient for national management of money flow. It provides an accurate picture of liquidity (the notorious M1, M2,

M3, ... money categories – reflecting lower degrees of liquidity): how much money is in checking accounts, how much in saving accounts, money markets, etc. But money on the phone is not so readily regulated, and its disposition, commitments, and liquidity is not open and apparent. Digital money crosses national borders with ease, and most alarming of all, digital money may cascade up to composite currencies.

Cascaded Digital Money

Let EuroDigit be a digital money denominated in euros, and DollarDigit – a currency in digital format – denominated in dollars. An enterprising business will combine the two and offer a EuroDollar digital money that is denominated in an artificial currency comprising one euro and one dollar per unit of EuroDollar. The digital format enables this fusing with no friction and no red-tape. For traders between these two continents, the EuroDollar may be found attractive because it is immunized against valuation seesaw between the constituent currencies. A second entrepreneur will throw the Chinese Yuan into the mix, and a fourth will add some silver and gold. As far as the payment mechanism goes, there is no difference between digital money denominated in dollars and one denominated in a basket of currencies. The basket comes with the advantage of diversification, stability, and better risk outlook. As currencies cascade up, they anchor on more and more of society's wealth, and the more so, the more stable they become. Instability rages when one element of our wealth (say, stocks) loses favor relative to another element (say, real estate). We may conclude then that a currency anchored on both stocks and real estate will be so much less volatile to changes in the relative attraction of the constituent elements. The more elements of wealth a currency is anchored on, the more stable it is. Stability being the most elemental property of money, such cascaded currency that climbs up to anchor on the totality of human wealth as a whole, will be inherently stable and fundamentally immunized against wild swings in value when the relative values of its building blocks undergo changes. The more stability such a cascaded currency will show, the more attractive it would be, the more popular too, and without much fanfare this currency will emerge as the de-facto global currency. This, of course, will not kill fiat currencies, as they would serve as the bases for the cascaded currency, and the better managed each fiat currency, the higher would rise its share in the cascaded global currency. The greater that share, the closer the cascaded currency behaves relative to the well-managed fiat currency.

But for the relevant central banks, to manage this newly emerging cascaded money is a challenge anew.

The Internet of Things, Avatars, and Robotics

In recent years, the stock market has been rocked by a new phenomenon: trading machines – computers reading feed data fractions of a second before the rest of the stock traders, and exploit this advantage through instant high-level transactions that sway the market beyond comfort. The stock market set out some rules to arrest this instability. Alas, this esoteric phenomenon is harbinger of a rising tsunami: devices, robots, avatars, or gadgets, networked through the Internet of Things are given the power to buy, sell, pay, and get paid – using mostly digital currency, digitized dollars, or euros, as the case may be. So suddenly, it's not only some hundreds of millions of humans spending money that the Federal Reserve need to control, add now countless "characters" – non-human entities loaded with artificial intelligence reasoning and creating huge financial turbulence. Unlike the fast stock trading, the machine transactions decisions cannot be banned; technology cannot be fenced in. For the central bankers, everywhere there would be no choice but to wrestle with the daily accumulated complexity and guide the national currency into comfortable stability, honoring all the other strategic aims all along.

Because digital money and tethered money are so nonlinear, so far off from payment and banking today, we run the risk that the powers that be, don't take the considerable amount of time necessary to learn and understand what technology offers. Executives may resign themselves to persistent ignorance of what comes down the pike, and respond with unhelpful caution and paralysis. It is always tempting to escape a difficult "what's next" decision by using a time shield: announcing a newly appointed study committee with a mandate to recommend solutions. The existence of such a committee proves that the politician is proactive, and provides him or her with a good answer to critics; all that without an apparent risk, who can fault a careful study?

Talking to high-level bankers in the past 2 years, I have encountered this reluctance to grab the bull by the horns. One executive admonished me: "Couldn't you wait 7 years until I retire! I have spent 10 years learning automatic clearing house, and now you want me to learn like in kindergarten, the new landscape of bits and bytes! Hey, smarty, if you are so innovative, creative, etc., why don't you cure cancer?"

MONEY: CHANGED BY CRYPTOGRAPHY

No sooner has money management sneaked into books and ledgers than the art and craft of cryptography was called in to render services. Books were encrypted, ledgers were enciphered, and, on the other side, books were decrypted, ledgers were cryptanalyzed, a match of wits took place. The battle between those who wish to hide their monetary affairs and those who wish to expose them only intensified when computers came into play. For one, it was so convenient to load up these new computing machines, and then let them do the hard work, formerly of human disposition. And for another, computers removed the money data into the bowels of these new mysterious machines wherein it was less visible whether secrets were compromised and data was stolen.

Albeit, that was the pale end of what was to come. The data that was used to account for the money that was actually transacted with physical coins, and tangible banknotes, has been upgraded to become the money itself. It happened gradually: money transactions were carried out without any exchange of a physical currency. This silent revolution was enabled by software. It worked as follows.

Alice buys from Bob[2] some merchandise and in return pays him, say, $10.00. The transaction happens "electronically" via phone/tablet/PC or alike. When done, it appears that money was flowing through the electronic veins of the Internet from Alice to Bob. But in fact what happened was that Alice's software communicated an instruction to Bob's software. The effect of the instruction was that the computer storage spot that houses the figure representing the amount of money credited to Bob was accessed, and the number therein was incremented by "10.00." In parallel, Alice's software accessed the computer storage spot that houses the number that represents Alice's credit and decreased its value by "10.00." A close-up look shows that no money was actually passed over from Alice to Bob. It was a signal to take actions: one action on Bob's side, and another on Alice's side.

This payment paradigm may be regarded as a wonderful abstraction: a passing software instruction replaces the tangible handover of a coin or a banknote. Money can flow anywhere software does, and safe boxes and vaults are replaced by computer addressable storage, holding a number. Beautiful indeed, alas also dangerous. It takes some effort to counterfeit a $100 federal note, but it is easy as pie to change the figure in a computer address – once you hacked your way into the computer. This software-based payment paradigm introduced unprecedented efficiency and unparalleled convenience but it also opened us to risks and attacks of a new class and of a new caliber of unprecedented dimensions.

It became plainly obvious that the only means at our disposal to enjoy the benefit of networking and computing in a world replete with thieves, cheats, and fraudsters is cryptography. Overnight, this arcane art that served esoteric spooks and off-the-beat spies has risen to become the technological pillar of modern day banking, payment, currency, and finance. Cryptographic protocols safeguard those computer storage places wherein money appears as binary numbers. Other cryptographic products accompany the software payment instructions that crisscross the Internet, and more crypto is applied to verify online identities, and prevent repudiation and denial of financial commitments.

Is It Working?

Are today's crypto-tools good enough to facilitate electronic commerce? Well, by and large, electronic payment systems are humming. Online commerce

---

2. Crypto-literature adopted this proverbial couple, Alice and Bob, to present cryptographic dialogs. One student told me that he met this nice young lady in the bar, who said that her name was Alice. "Oh, dear Alice!" he exclaimed. "You have no idea how many long hours I have been thinking of you!" He had a hard time explaining to Alice that what she thought of as a tasteless pick-up line was in fact his dire reality in Professor Samid's crypto class.

claims a bigger share of worldwide transactions year after year. The paradigm of software-based instruction exchange has proven its merit several times over. Yes, it looks fine and dandy but the Barbarians are at the gate. We hope that the cryptographic tools that we use are good and robust, but we are not sure. We have no proof, only "hope." We also hope that our adversaries will not think of something we have missed, but we have no reason to be confident of this assumption either. We keep integrating the payment nodes (banks, processors, credit networks, mobile networks) into larger and larger interdependent financial assemblies. Modern complexity science assures us that risk of collapse increases exponentially with the size of the integrated system, but the lure of convenience, speed, and instant efficiency is too much to resist. Our dependence on crypto-protected software-based electronic payment is increasing daily; the later the point of breakdown, the bigger the prospective disruption.

Against this backdrop and its inherent risks, a novel concept emerged: *digital money.*

Aren't we digital already? The computer-stored figures that represent money today are in fact binary strings – *digital.* So why do we refer to *"digital money"* as something new and unprecedented?

A $1.00 bill is an entity that carries its value – written on its face: one dollar, but it also represents a particular instance of a dollar, different from the next $1.00 bill. Two-dollar bills may be bundled together or be kept apart. Alice may pass one bill to Bob and keep the other. The bills, in fact, have an identifying serial number that is unique. In other words, the $1.00 bill or the $1.00 coin *reflects both value and identity.*

By contrast (and that is crucial), the bit string in the computer storage that says $1.00 is only a declaration of value – not of identity. The fundamental reason for our cyber vulnerability today is this innocent sounding fact: the money today is expressed as a generic value, without any mark of identity. It is this very fact that allows a hacker to sneak into the computer and alter the figure from $1.00 to $100.00 or to whatever he wishes.

The novel idea that we are talking about is to rectify this fundamental vulnerability; to represent money digitally in a way wherein both the face value and the identity of the money are carried digitally. We are looking therefore, at a binary string, say: "01101011001110011001001" that represents both a value and a "bill" identifier. The mint of this string will keep a record of its minted money and will acknowledge as valid only such strings that it actually minted. That means that if a hacker drills his way into the computer storage spot wherein such digital money bill is kept, he would not be able to alter $1.00 to $100.00 because his arbitrary substitution will not be redeemable.

"Wait a minute," one will challenge: "But the hackers might zero in on the mint and hack its data!" Yes, they will, but then we have only the mint to protect. Today every unremarkable computer anywhere, with money on it, can be hacked. It's much better to draw the battle lines around the mint and fight it out on our chosen turf.

The last point deserves elaboration: today's battle lines are long and convoluted. Hackers have the luxury of choosing a single weak link and hack through. They may start stealing money right there. Or, they may exploit their penetration to secure credentials with which to penetrate to another bank, with better security. Only that this security will not be triggered because the hackers slide in with the credentials of the first bank. From the second, the hacker will climb to the third bank, and so on. The results explode on our daily news, with the latest: $1 billion cyber heist. Using digital money the hacker will be forced into our chosen place – the mint, wherein our best guns and our best defense is deployed.

The original lure of digital currency – currency expressed digitally and including a unique identifier – was the desired attribute of anonymity.

In today's software-based transaction paradigm, Alice and Bob will have to identify whom they are talking to. Bob cannot increment the number in the storage place that carries his credit without having assurances that the instruction to do so came from a known and trusted source. Indeed, in today's e-commerce, anonymity is nearly impossible. Now there are some clever ways around it, using proxy, etc., but essentially the software exchange protocol requires mutual identification. By contrast, digital money in the form presented above does carry its own value, and it matters not how its holder achieved possession thereof. Bob will not have to verify that it was Alice and not Nancy that sent him the digital dollar bill because if the identifier is bona fide, the digital string is good for its face value, much like in regular cash transactions. You buy merchandise for cash, without revealing your identity.

The lure of anonymity in cyber world was, and is, a big draw, and several attempts to develop a robust digital currency were attempted. As of today, none of these attempts grabbed a hold in the financial mainstream. The reasons are mainly (1) security and (2) off-currency.

Security

Developers of digital currency simply migrated the cryptographic tools used to safeguard communication and applied them to safeguard digital currency. This strategy is a failing strategy regardless of which algorithms are chosen or how cleverly they are applied. The reason being is that all the mainstay ciphers and crypto-algorithms in use today are of unknown intractability (complexity, difficulty to crack) and well-established intractability erosion. That means they lose their defense as time passes. We don't know how fast these algorithms weaken but, then again, we don't even know whether our smartest adversaries have already cracked our mainstay crypto-algorithms, and they are careful enough to keep this fact a secret, the way the Allies did not brag on cracking the German Enigma, in World War II, but hid this fact, at great cost. If we come to suspect at some point that our current flagship, the advanced encryption standard (AES) cipher, has been compromised, we will drop it right away, and in no time use some AES-II for our subsequent communication. But the situation is different with digital currency. Suppose we invented a digital currency based on AES, and our invention spreads like brush fire, billions and billions of dollars have been digitized and used for storage and payment, all protected by AES intractability. And then, one bright day, some teenager from Iceland posts on his Facebook page a clever mathematical insight to crack AES. From that moment on, any AES-protected money loses its validity. In other words, cracking and compromising a foundational cipher that represents money and wealth will instantly melt away all the outstanding credit and monetary assets, so based, across the globe. We don't need much imagination to conclude that this would be a Biblical size judgment day. So DigiCash, and Bitcoin, and everything in between may be viable candidates for limited use, but for a sense of what is to come – much as the various attempts to fly before the Wright brothers, were very instructional and provided critical lessons toward the first successful airplane. Alas, a scalable, robust digital money solution must be pursued with a different strategy.

The Off-Currency

Alarmingly, the complex system of hundreds of millions of psychology-afflicted human beings, each deciding for himself and herself whether to honor the dollar or not, sums up to a questionable stability. We are too ignorant about individual decision making, not to speak about crowd behavior, to be sure that this stability will continue tomorrow. In particular, we are not sure that some dollar-alternative offered to the American people will not grab the fancy of the multitude and carry us to uncharted territories. So, one thing for sure, any challenger currency that rises above obscurity becomes enemy of the state. The state has not only computers, the state has guns. And yes, it would be "brute force" but it would be unleashed. The only practical hope to sustain a steady global growth of a digital currency is to digitize the currency of the state.

Amazingly, the most powerful, most revolutionary feature of digital money was left largely unrecognized until now.

MONEY: TETHERED

Consider the following tuple:

$$[Face\ value] - [Unique\ identifier] - [Terms\ of\ payment]$$

By referring to face value as V, the unique identifier as I, and the terms of payment as T, this association of these three pieces of data (tuple) becomes

$$V - I - T$$

This simple association offers the key for a revolution that defies today's imagination to describe even its contours.

What make this tuple interesting is that it is unique. There is not a tuple like this anywhere. If Alice wishes to pay Bob the sum of $V = \$100$ each week for 5 weeks, she could not change the value of V in the tuple from $\$100$ to $\$200$, $\$300$, etc. Rather she will have to remit five tuples: $\$100–I_1–T$, $\$100–I_2–T$, $\$100–I_3–T$, ... The term, T, could be the same, but don't have to be. The sum, V, is the same, but also don't have to be. For sure, though, the identification string, I, for each tuple (coin) will be different. The tuple carries the value of $\$100$, but it is a unique instance of $\$100$, and this particular instance of $\$100$ is inexorably tied to T – terms of payments, or say, terms of redemption. If T is satisfied, then the coin redeemer may exchange it with another instance of $\$100$ that has no redemption restrictions: $\$100–I'–[T = 0]$. The new instance has a different ID. The redeemer could also redeem the tuple against an old-fashioned $\$100$ paper bill.

Such a tuple is realized as a combined bit string $[V–I–T]$, which expresses a monetary value, V, a unique bill identity, I, and an inexorably linked redemption terms, T. *We say then that this bill, identified as I, of denominated value V is tethered to terms of redemption T.* One could claim its return $\$V$, if, and only if, the terms, T are fully satisfied. Otherwise, the mint that issued (minted) this tuple will not redeem it. In other words, only by complying with the logical conditions spelled out in T will it be possible to render the coin of $\$V$ value into "regular (untethered) money." Money so constructed, a tuple so minted, is regarded and defined as "tethered money."

There are cryptographic means to insure that a tuple (coin) owner cannot simply erase or modify the terms of payment (or the ID for that matter), but at any rate, the mint that constructed this tuple and put it in circulation will have a copy thereto in its redemption database.

Quick minds will develop a thousand questions, such as: could Bob deduce the cryptographic key that protects the integrity of the tuple, could he steal the key, or replace it; could Bob hack into Alice's computer and add a fake coin to her database; could Bob build a fake $V–I–T$ tuple such that it would encrypt into the same cryptographic signature used to identify the tuple integrity? And the most fundamental question: can Bob redeem the tuple twice, or more?

All these questions are valid, serious, and must be answered to one's complete satisfaction but, alas, to answer them would take us off the main track of this book, so we can refer the reader to the reference list in this book for further reading, and here simply state in summary that these cryptographic questions do have good operational answers, and in fact Alice could construct a $V–I–T$ tuple, and hand it out to Bob against a payment of $\$V$ (Alice then plays the role of a mint). Bob may pass the tuple on, and it may be carried out and exchanged among many traders, until at some point the tuple is returned to Alice and, if the terms in T are satisfied, then Alice will make the payment to the person or entity that submitted the tuple for redemption.

T, the terms of payment, may be any logical statement. Some typical terms are as follows:

- Anonymity – first and second degree
- Identity of the redeemer
- Window of time for redemption
- Event reference
- Interest rate
- History

One of the most powerful and attractive features of digital money is the aspect of anonymity. The terms of reference would be able to indicate: *"pay to whoever submits this coin for redemption – ask for no identity, and don't ask any identity-revealing questions."* Such coin can be passed to anyone, be she a bosom friend or be he a total stranger. That anonymous coin can be lost, stolen, and robbed, and the finder, the thief, and the robber will be able to claim its face value because the terms of payment so indicate. Alternatively, the terms may specify anonymity of the second degree. Accordingly, the redeemed sum will be held by the mint in trust for a preset amount of time (minutes, days, … more). If no one tries to redeem the same coin during that time interval, the coin is redeemed to its sole claimant – whoever he or she is. If two or more claim the very same coin, then the mint will initiate a conflict-resolution procedure. For example, each claimant will have to finger the source that provided him or her with the disputed coin. There are various cryptographic primitives that would allow Alice to point to Bob as the payer of a digital coin – without Bob realizing who he is providing with such a proof. It's somewhat like writing a receipt for a cash buyer. This procedure is designed to flash out who traded for the coin and who stole it.

The identity of the redeemer may be a uniquely named individual, a specific passkey holder individual, or perhaps a member-of-a-class individual. For example, the redeemer may be defined as anyone that works for a given corporation, or any resident of some small city. Any unambiguous logical condition could identify individuals eligible to redeem any given tuple (digital coin).

Money given as a construction loan may be limited for redemption only by qualified contractors to insure that the borrower is not spending the money in Vegas.

Tethered money may be redeemable from a certain date to a certain date. A renter could use such coins to pay his rent a year ahead, and specify for each coin the next month as the window of redemption for that coin.

Money can be redeemable only after a specified event occurs, or, say, before an event takes place. The event may be any well-defined occurrence, or perhaps an approval signature of some relevant authority.

Interest Rate

One of the most exciting uses of digital money is to use it while collecting interest on it. The interest rate will be specified to be added to the redemption sum. In some other cases, the mint provides all sorts of special services for which it collects interest (negative interest from the standpoint of the redeemer).

History

A coin may be set for redemption only if it carries with it its entire history. Using any of a variety of cryptographic solutions, a coin may be associated with a proven track record of who was in possession thereto from the moment it was minted to the moment it is being redeemed. If the chain of custody is broken, the coin is not redeemable.

The terms of payment associated with each digital coin may be much more complicated, much more imaginative, much more powerful than the basic types discussed here. Anything that can be algorithmically checked and verified with no ambiguity is a bona fide term of payment.

MONEY: AN INNOVATION TURTLE

No sooner have our ancestors emerged from their nomadic culture, and settlements have been established in Southeast Asia, in Mesopotamia, in Egypt, than the grand idea of barter and exchange took hold. Barter was the prevailing method of exchange for perhaps as long as 4000 years. The notion of "money" as a universal medium of exchange, store of value, and unit of accounting, was slow in coming. The earliest record for the seed of this far-reaching idea is from about 3000 BC in Egypt and Mesopotamia. Gold bars, measures of agricultural grains, were used then for the same purpose for which we today pull out our credit card. The next innovative step is recorded 2300 years later, at around 700 BC, when the innovative people of Aegina came up with the dramatic innovation of a government stamped coins – *the drachma*. What a relief! No need to drag around a scale, and argue where the needle is. All you needed to do was to count. You inspected the stamp, were satisfied by its authenticity, and it was as good as gold. No different from coin handling today, including the future hybrid coins. The practice of replacing primary money with paper receipts serving as proof that primary money is redeemable against them was a gradual development, where over a very long time these notes became more official and more standardized. Money by decree (fiat) was practiced in ancient Rome, but only as late as 1971 President Nixon reinstituted the US dollar as a fiat currency, backed by itself only.

Money innovation proceeds with a turtle pace. *Will tethered money break that mold?*

The reason for this lengthy introduction of digital tethered money is that it is important to understand this novel entity before delving into the ocean of exciting applications that are based on it.

"CATCH ME IF YOU CAN": THE ULTIMATE CURRENCY WAR

The aftermath of 9-11 highlighted a big difference between the Cold War and the war in the new "world order." The new enemy was without a clear retaliation target: distributed, hidden, and elusive. There was no Moscow to dial in its coordinates into the powerful Intercontinental Ballistic Missiles (ICBM); there was no clear frontline like between Western Europe and the Soviet Union. The most eligible retaliation target President Bush could think of was Afghanistan for hosting the Al-Qaeda camps. The proponents of bitcoin are hoping for the same advantage. An algorithm is not locked to an office into which FBI SWAT teams may barge. A protocol hovers everywhere, with no clear place of residence to blow out of existence. So, furious as the US government and other governments may be, they can't "kill" bitcoin, so claim the war like challengers, and despite desperate attempts by the powers that be, the trade with bitcoin or a bitcoin-like currency will prevail, so the argument goes.

Indeed, using encryption and smart protocols, traders could practice bitcoin transactions that remain arguably undetected. The DarkNet – the under-side of the Internet – is proof that the bad guys can communicate and trade unchecked by law enforcement. The famous "Silk Road" site run by Ross Ulbricht became a very busy cyber market for illicit drugs, murders for hire, human trafficking, and even terrorism. The currency of choice was bitcoin. The FBI claimed that a momentary online mistake by Mr Ulbricht led them to bust the site and its trade. The FBI admitted that the Silk Road traders immediately found a different venue. The underlying concepts of DarkNet are simple and robust. It is based on protocols developed by the US Navy ... (TOR). If Alice and Bob wish to conduct an illicit transaction, then it is not enough for them to hide the contents of their deeds; they need to conceal the fact that they communicate with each other. If Joe from Chicago is busy talking with a known illicit drug dealer in Columbia, then even if his communication is not busted, he draws attention to himself. The DarkNet provides anonymization protocols based on the concept of "onion layers." Alice sends a message to Carla, which she decrypts only to the point needed to know that she has to forward that message to David. David will decrypt it to read his next target, etc. Neither Carla, nor David, and not the FBI know that Bob is the ultimate target for Alice. If Bob pays for Alice goods with bitcoins, then even Alice can't betray his identity because she does not have it.

So will bitcoin prevail and flood the market to the point that the old greenback will fade away? Hardly. The lack of harsh enforcement against bitcoin today is because bitcoin is so negligible in volume. But no sooner would bitcoin, or a bitcoin-like currency, rise to a threat level, then the DarkNet will be busted. It's not easy, but not impossible. Bitcoin anonymity is based on an ingenious protocol of private/public keys that allow two strangers in cyberspace to establish a confidential channel of communication even though everything that they say to each other is carefully monitored. The subtle vulnerability of this protocol is the fact that it does not guarantee Alice that she talks to Bob. It only guarantees to her that she establishes a secure communication channel with whom she started the protocol. This subtle distinction will allow an FBI agent to carefully and timely hop in, pose as Bob, and secure the confidential channel with Alice, leading to busting her secrecy.

And if everything else fails, if bitcoin, crime, or terrorism ever succeeds to outsmart the good guys, and turn the Internet into a winning weapon against the public good, then governments still have the weapon of last resort: the routers, the physical lines, and the power supply cannot be whisked away in a suitcase, nor buried without a trace. The government can shut down the Internet, then restart it under a new harsh regimen. It would be a sad milestone in the history of humanity, if the sun ever rises on such a day, but one should keep it in mind.

CONSPIRACY THEORIES

True to form the bitcoin blogosphere is replete with extreme, paranoid, and out of this world theories as to what it is all about, and who is behind it. The fact that the author of record of bitcoin, Satoshi Nakamoto, is a mystery, only fans the flames of percolating minds. One such theory claims that bitcoin was planted on earth by some nihilists, or a rogue government with the plan to lure humanity to trust the bitcoin algorithms, and then, at the right moment, the instigators will publish the cracking algorithms, and all that wealth will be vaporized. I guess someone, somewhere may think that this is a good thing …

These feverish theories serve us a lesson. Money is way too potent, too delicate, too consequential an issue to let it be guided by anything less than our best combination of wisdom and experience.

Chapter 2

Tethered Money: Use and Impact

Chapter Outline

The invention of money offered people greater control of their lives, which became the opening for great and wonderful inventions and cultural evolutions. There are good grounds to project that the technology of tethered money would further increase the measure of control over lives and resources, maturing our civilization into wonderful places, only the most basic thereto do we have the power to imagine. The technology of tethered money effectively combats waste, fraud, and abuse. Its spectrum is dramatically broad: from welfare, unemployment, Medicaid, grants, endowments, to more effective management, more productive research and development, more control over government spending, management of loyalty money, rewards and coupons, implementing innovative healthcare, upgrading the credit market, micropayments, nanopayments, media distribution, pay-as-you-go ... still, the lion share of what's to come has not yet been imagined.

We shall introduce this central question of use and impact by first discussing some straightforward cases, and subsequently delving into the more profound impact of the technology.

Tethered Money: Managing Digital Currency Transactions. http://dx.doi.org/10.1016/B978-0-12-803477-4.00002-8

EARNED VERSUS GRANTED

When nominal money emerged in our ancestral society, it was very hard to foresee that its existence would allow society to practice a certain efficiency that would, in due time, prove to be the central practice that underlies human progress. Money, stored value, enabled the practice of division of labor. Different folks did different works. The farmer could store the money he got for his harvest to buy fish from the fisherman who returned from his fishing trip 3 months later. Without division of labor, we all had to be carbon copies of each other, more or less. As indicated in the opening of this book, money that enabled division of labor, also enabled all the human inventions that shaped up our society. Without division of labor, these inventors would have had to labor in the field to grow their own wheat, and construct their own house. Money, stored value, allowed these inventors to dedicate their time to their invention. Division of labor not only benefited the genius inventors of old, but rather every one with a work product of a longer time span. Constructing a bridge, a boat, or a carriage, amounts to a long-lasting project, but the project workers have to eat everyday. Someone has to accumulate enough stored value – money – to feed the crew, to build the implements that, in turn, bring about progress.

Over the centuries, the cascade of all those technological inventions increased human productivity several folds. In early society, most people were farmers, few were ironsmiths, or of few other professions, but today a "handful" of farmers in the Midwest section of the United States are capable of feeding almost the entire planet. Modern economy evolved into high productivity enterprise, operated by a small, highly educated workforce. This dramatic change created a large class of dependents. They comprise youngsters who are on the receiving end for the first two decades of their lives; retired elderly who live longer and longer, and are treated with more and more expensive modern medicine, to keep living beyond all past measures; a multitude of adults lacking the necessary skills to fit into the demanding workforce; waves of immigrants, legal and illegal, drawn to the rich West from the third world.

This book is too narrow a frame to fully address the sociopolitical implications of this imbalance. Two aspects are important for our case here. The first is that having a great number of people relieved from the grind of insuring bare survival may become a leverage to committing human attention to growth, arts, science, research, and accelerated pace of the evolution of life and humanity. The second relates to the growing number of people on the receiving end. "An idle mind is the workshop of the devil." The weird, the evil, the fanatic may rise from the crowds that are "free to roam." It's only natural for rationalization to turn things around, and develop some straw man philosophy to acclaim the recipients and shame the producers. Much as the population that owes its security to the few who volunteer to join the armed forces, often derides those few. Those whose labor supports the rest should be acknowledged for their contribution, and a distinction in their favor should be the practice of a grateful society.

These two points are nicely addressed through the technology of tethered money. Money given not against an equal measure of goods and services provided at present may be subject to restrictions – tethering. Money that is paid for an equal measure of desired goods and services should be free of tethering. In other words, society should tether unearned money and untether earned money. It is just and proper for the government to cut a welfare check to those who need it, but tether that money to a sphere of use that excludes, for example, casino gambling, pleasure cruise, and purchase of fine jewelry. We should all justify parents restricting the use of their allowance, and OK the restriction for proper use of research grants, etc. By contrast, a factory worker salary will be totally untethered, unrestricted. Same for the money paid to a work contractor, a physician, a lawyer, a cobbler, or a plumber who exchanges goods and services against the money paid to them. In many practical instances, the distinction will be purely psychological but nonetheless very important. Peter was laid off and received government assistance from various agencies to the tune of $3500/month. His neighbor, Paul, works in a store and his salary is $3500/month. The two neighbors spend their money alike, but Paul enjoys the sensation of freedom to use his money any way he pleases, no restrictions, no tethering, whereas Peter has to stay within the confines of his tethered support money. Using tethered money technology, the government does not need law enforcement to make sure that Peter abides by his restriction. His digital cash melts away any time he tries to use it where he should not. Although Paul's digital coins can buy him anything priced for the money in his possession – no restriction. Clearly Paul is proud of his untethered funds, and Peter is envious – in a good way, envy that should lead to determination to rise to the station where he has some goods and services worth payment in free untethered money.

In other words, the new technology of tethered money creates a healthy, fair, and motivation breeding distinction between the shrinking sector who gets paid earned, untethered money, and the growing sector that is paid unearned, tethered funds.

INVESTMENT

Societies increasingly realized that taking a long view is advantageous, which means that some members of society will have to be "gambled on" – paid so they can live – for a long time until their work produces results that justify this investment. But this leads to a reality where money is poured and paid against no clear indications of good use. The recipients of such money can hardly be expected to withstand the temptation to falsely assure the payer that due progress is happening, whereas, in fact, progress is lagging because the received money is subtly misdirected to more immediate self-serving rewards. And one can hardly fault the payers in these circumstances when they hold back on many projects, not sure whether they are being deceived and progress reports are exaggerated. This reality leads to, on one hand, less then diligent pursuit of such long-term programs, and on the other hand, less than totally generous investment in same long-term project targets.

Here too, both problems are rooted in the universality of money. As money has no smell, no clear origin, no history, and no built-in restrictions, it is readily misallocated, misapplied, and misused by the recipients of such long-term programs. Tethered money would cut into this abuse by insuring that the unearned money paid to people involved in long-term projects would be strictly used on these projects. And once investors are so reassured they will be more generous, and less apprehensive in putting their money on the long-range bet. And the more we bet on long-term enterprise, the more progress we may expect.

Investment tethering may tie payments to pace of progress, expert approval, selected suppliers, purchased items, and any combination thereto. Any logical restriction will work. In fact, the full specification of the governing investment contract can be mapped into a tethered investment. All the restrictions, conditions, and obligations may be expressed as tethered coins.

Why bother? If the terms of the investment are fully spelled out in the governing contract, why duplicate that contract into tethered money? After all, if a contract is being deviated from, then some remedies kick in to make the victim whole. Indeed so, but what a drain: you have to keep comparing the contract to what happens in the field. And there is the issue of interpretation, opinion, argument, and discussions back and forth. Then come the threats of lawsuit, first verbal, then written. If all else fails, a lawsuit must be filed. Anyone who ever was a party to a lawsuit, needs no graphic description of what a headache this is. Compare this tedium to the simplicity of tethered money. Using the services of tethered digital money mint – the funds are nonusable if they don't comply with the tethered conditions. It is one thing to invoke remedies and undo damage from misspent funds; it is a different and easier world altogether to prevent the abuse, the spending in the first place. Tethering seems to bend the case toward the investor, and against the executor. Indeed so because the risk is assumed by the investor. The investor lays out money against expectations, not against at-present counter conveyance of goods and services. Suppose an investor writes out three big coins each tethered to a successive milestone in the project. Yes, it assures the investor that the contractor will not spend the money prematurely, but it also assures the contractor that the funds are there to keep the project going.

MANAGEMENT

Tethered money will allow managers to write their spending rules and payment protocols into the money itself, and so insure that it would not be paid without complying with the stated rules. This, by itself, will relieve management from the detailed follow-up, extensive bookkeeping, and worry about the honesty of members of the team. Oftentimes business managers agree to pay a sum in installments. This can be readily accomplished with money tethering. Each installment will be tied to a time interval in which it can be redeemed. Tethering will allow managers to delegate spending and payment authority while maintaining good overall control. This is because different individuals in the business will be in control of money that is tethered according to their responsibility in the business.

Tethering is forwardly constructive, which means that an owner of a digital coin can add tethers to it, as he passes it on to its next recipient. An owner cannot deconstruct a tether (no backward adjustment), but there is no limit to the add-on tethering. Illustration: an investor tethers his project investment by tethering it to a list of vendors and subcontractors. That means that money can only be redeemed by anyone on that list. The project manager receiving that money will further allocate a portion thereof to a subordinate manager and further restrict that money to be used as payment to only two suppliers from the first list. Of course, the project manager cannot designate a supplier from outside his (first) list because that would violate the coin tethering. The subordinate manager might further parcel out the resources allocated to him, and give a portion thereto to a purchasing supervisor to use only for purchasing construction materials (not tools) from only one of the two suppliers that she was constrained to. In short, various management levels within the project organizations are using the tethering tool to facilitate their management, keep track of expenses, and spare the need to constantly check and follow-up, compare actual to what is written in the contract. The mint simply operates as the all-level "law enforcement" or "management instruction enforcement." An alternative configuration will allow retethering without involving the mint, by using surrogate mints and subcontracted tethering.

Tethering Visibility Management

When tethering is applied to a project management environment where payments require various managerial approvals, one could set up a visibility management scheme, so that manager Alice will see whether manager Bob approved the payment before she decides on her position, whereas manager Bob will not be able to see whether manager Carla has approved the payment, so he is not influenced by this fact. In situations where independent judgment is required the approving managers should be mutually invisible, but in cases where one relies, say, on expert opinions, visibility is essential. The digital coin itself will carry along these exacting visibility distinctions.

Tethering Flexibility

The logical evaluation of the tethering status may take the full complexity and flexibility offered by any computerized logic. For example, nominally, say, a tethered coin will be redeemed if Alice, Bob, and Carla all approve it for payment. A flexible version will state that if any two of them approve, then the coin will be redeemed. Or, say, if six people are listed as approvers of the payment, the logic may state that if any four of them approve, the coin is redeemed or if Alice and anyone else of the remaining five approve the redemption, it goes. Tethering may also handle range designations. For example, a coin is redeemable if Alice appraises the work, for which the coin is paid, to be complete. Alternatively, Alice will be asked to grade her satisfaction from the work on a scale from 1 (lowest) to 5 (highest), and the logic will indicate that on a satisfaction grade "3" or higher the coin is redeemable.

SURROGATE MINT/SUBCONTRACTED TETHERING

The mint is the natural administrator for tethering; however, in any financial environment tethering services may be subcontracted. The mint might feature one tethering requirement: an approval by Alice. Alice then would set up tethering requirements to her heart's content, and latch the cryptographic expression of these conditions and requirements to the digital coin issued by the mint. Alice will then be responsible for the integrity and robustness of these cryptographic means, and she will then serve as a surrogate mint. Bob, Carla, David, etc., who would receive their tethered coins from Alice will have eventually to satisfy her in order to untether their money. The mint will be blind to these add-on tethering latched by Alice to its coin. Bob or Carla would not be able to go behind Alice's back and redeem the coin from the mint because the mint looks for Alice's "Ok to pay" signal. Only when Alice is satisfied that her layer of tethering has been fulfilled, will she stamp her cryptographic OK on the coin, and allow Bob, Carla, etc., to get their money. Of course Bob, on his part, could latch to the coin his own set of tethering requirements so that he can better manage Eve and Fred who work for him. Alice will be blind to Bob's tethering much as the mint is blind to hers. These layering of surrogate mints can be reapplied indefinitely. It might be very helpful in a large multilayered project environment. A built-in advantage to this configuration is that the integrity of the money and all the payments hinges on the underlying mint. Bob, Carla, Fred, or any other person or entity involved will be able to check with the mint that the bit-string given to them by Alice or others is indeed of monetary value. The mint will pacify Fred, and say, for example, yes, the string you showed us is worth $1000. Now, we cannot redeem it for you because we don't show Alice's approval for the payment, but the value is there.

INNOVATION

Innovation has tiptoed itself into the seat of power and reverence formerly held by kings and religions. Future historians might consider innovation to be the religion of the twenty-first century. When we are in a bind, we look for some innovative ideas to help us out; when we face a challenge, we trust that we can soon think of something we did not think of before. When we write our history, we list the innovations and inventions that transformed our lives. Innovation is universal, exciting, uplifting; innovation is a source of answers – all the critical attributes of religion are there, with one exception. Innovation demands newness not repetitiveness. Individual survival, corporate survival, and national survival are all focused on innovation.

Oftentimes though, innovation is seen as primarily a matter of creativity. To be innovative one has to think afresh, imagine out-of-the-box, disrupt linear progress, and conceive things out of the blue. Indeed so, creativity is a must, albeit, not sufficient. It's not creativity and the pure notion of innovation that transform our lives and move our culture forward. It's innovation productivity. Millions of excellent ideas in the inventor's drawer are feeding no hungry child and curing no single patient. Innovative ideas need to be worked on, developed, tried, tested, adjusted, and, yes, on many occasions, dropped. All this development, trying, testing, adjusting, etc., is costly. And hence innovation productivity requires both creativity and allocated resources.

But as so many innovative ideas end up dropped or abandoned, and many other end up limping with reality being a fraction of their initial vision, the people that hold the purse string are naturally very apprehensive. "Sure, a good innovative idea is the best investment there is!" investors agree. "But so many bad innovative ideas do a good job masquerading as a good one," they add wistfully.

Tethered money cannot do away with the built-in uncertainties of an innovation environment, but it has the power to clarify, and the power to reduce that uncertainty to the inherent minimum by eliminating the issues that arise because of human imperfection.

As alluded before, innovators operating with other people's money will be tempted to put a smoke screen over the reality of the project. They may be crooks and willfully steer money for other aims, or they may be inefficient and spend money on dead-end research strategies. Some, unfortunately, combine these two unpraiseworthy attributes. Think what that will do! This smoke screen phenomenon is well realized by the sponsors of the research. Venture capitalists generally observe that somehow the first 90% of project progress happen ahead of schedule, only the last 10% of progress takes forever ... The strategy of the recipient of the investment is self-serving: to keep the investor happy for as long as possible, using glowing (misleading) reports regarding progress. When the bitter truth eventually comes out, the investor is deeply committed, he or she has too much to lose, if they cut the project off, and begrudgingly they keep funding. Although this may work for the short run, it certainly chills the atmosphere for that investor and that recipient for the next projects.

The reality today in the United States, and less so in Europe, is that once a research and development proposal is approved, the money flows even if everyone knows that the progress report is pure fiction. Say then that in reality, the innovation industry is plagued by the inherent uncertainty of the innovative challenge, with the added uncertainty of the conduct of the people that run the innovation enterprise. Replacing this reality with tethered funding will all but eliminate the human conduct uncertainty and keep the innovation going with the inherent uncertainty alone.

Innovation tethering technically is similar to investment tethering and management tethering discussed earlier. Only that tethering for innovation is of greater urgency. Our growing list of potential calamities and affliction on humanity in general can only be met with aggressive and productive innovation. Tethered innovation funding will help keep the innovation practitioners on track and efficient, and will encourage the critical sponsors of innovation to put more into this avenue. Tethered money technology will also allow for new innovative funding avenues to support productive innovation.

If Thomas Edison would have needed to beg for money for his research into better lighting fixtures, his way to get the money would have been to write an elaborate proposal for investigating new and innovative wax materials to make candles burn longer, with less dripping. Once the money was in, he could have steered it to his crazy idea of using electrical current inside a vacuum glass. That is the norm for many of today's academic researchers. The reason being that some obscure cadres of mavens decide what we will know tomorrow. These deciders naturally support the money interests that commission them. People, on their part, could email tethered funds to a researcher of their choice, to advance a topic they are interested in. There is ample room for creativity. A grass root commission of experts, say on Alzheimer, may spring up spontaneously, and call upon people to send tethered funds to Alzheimer researchers they approve of. Researchers, in turn, will have more options of committees to shop around to validate their research plan.

GOVERNMENT

The US Federal government manages the largest enterprise ever on the face of the earth. Very few people at the very top oversee an enormous complexity. Two processes are essential for this challenge: one is a faithful summary reporting of what is going on, and the other is a faithful detailed interpretation of the summary directions issued by the top brass. Unfortunately, both processes are inundated with imperfections, and to that extent the management process is wasteful, abusive, and even fraudulent.

The imperfections in both processes are a result of a power struggle between the top echelon of government – the policy writers, and the middle core of entrenched career managers that assemble the summaries and execute the policies. The latter view the former as ephemeral, transient, not very knowledgeable of the subject matter, in short, politicians. The middle managers, the bureaucrats, finesse the reporting, and skew interpret the policy instructions. The top echelon doesn't have the staff, and often not the inclination to follow-up on the fidelity of either process.

Tethered money is in a clear position to help the policy makers enforce their will on the carry out level. Today, the budget allocation is exercised with universal money, which the bureaucrats can shuffle to their liking using the flimsiest of excuses. The same funds can be handed over to the bureaucrat as tethered funds, where the tethering reflects the exact policy dictates discerned by the upper tier. Senators, Congresspersons, even department heads will not have to dig into mired details, or search among purposefully confusing reports, the money itself will be inexorably tied to its declared purpose, minute and detailed as it may be. The power to interpret broad-brush policy orders, now held in the hands of the bureaucrats, will return to the elected representatives of the American people. And as the elected representatives are accountable to the people, this power shift is welcome.

It is important to state that tethered money, however minute, will offer management *help*, but will be far from a panacea. Bureaucrats are well skilled in what is referred to as creative accounting. Say the budget calls for construction of a new library, but the county council fancies a colorful water fountain to attract tourists (and which is commissioned to the daughter-in-law of the county executive), so they would recast the fountain as a library annex, and pay for it from the library funds. Today, they shuffle discreet amounts from budget items that are not very well defined, are hard to assess, and for which no one complaints if the spending is less. With tethered money such budget allocation is impossible, so it's more difficult to deviate, to fudge, to cheat.

It may be worth repeating the answer to the natural question: what is the difference between tethered money so described and top management issuing a high-resolution allocation plan for the budgeted money, requiring a detailed report of expenditures. It is the difference between asking moviegoers to show their admission ticket before they get in and to collecting the admission fee on their way out. What would the movie theater do with dozens of moviegoers who claim they spent their last dime on popcorn? Yes, they could file dozens of lawsuits, invite the police, etc., but in practice they would do nothing of the sort. Similarly, with request for detailed reports, the people on the execution side simply don't write that report, with little risk of a meaningful penalty. And if they write it, they keep it long, confusing, unreadable, and get away with it. And the money was spent, or misspent anyway, what good would a report do? Tethered money, by contrast, does not get spent before its terms are met. It's like the would-be moviegoers who don't get to see the movie without producing the ticket.

The Tax Code

The US Federal tax code is a monument of complexity.[1] Many are trying to simplify it to no avail. The reason is that the code is the main tool applied by the US Congress for its social engineering goals. For example, the department of energy wishes to encourage people to use solar energy, so they get Congress to write into the tax code, some special discounts and credits for anyone installing solar receptors on his roof.

The government wishes to encourage home ownership versus renting, so it allows deduction mortgage interest payments. Legislators are worried about longer living Americans who have no savings to sustain them, so they exempt some income from taxation if that income is allocated to a retirement program.

The coming reality of tethered money will offer an alternative. The US government could announce that it would issue $4750 of money tethered to solar receptors. This tethered money will be sold to the public against $4000 of untethered money. In other words, the government will sell tethered money against a lower sum of untethered money. Every citizen could opt for this exchange. Accounting-wise, this offer is equivalent to the government issuing a $750 tax rebate. But what a difference! The way it is done today, the government resorts to trust the tax returns of the claimants, only a tiny fraction of them gets audited. With tethered money, the policing is shifted to the mint. The solar tethered money is no good for Vegas, even for groceries. It is only usable for its tethered

---

1. "With its 6000 pages and 500 million words, the complexity of our tax code is the prime source of frustration and anger felt by millions of Americans toward their government." US Representative Spencer Bachus (R-AL).

purpose: purchasing of solar panels. Only a supplier of those panels will be able to redeem this tethered money with the mint. The government, on its part, once it sold the tethered cash to the citizen, is out of it, nothing to monitor or examine. The citizen who was party to this exchange may either use it for the indicated purpose, or lose it. The government could issue a limited number of such tethered "coins" on a first come, first serve basis. The tethered money may even come with an expiration date, or any other logical add-on term.

There are countless ways to carry out "social engineering" missions. The government could offer solar panel manufacturers a lower income tax rate for income generated from tethered money. This would motivate the manufacturers to offer their clients company-tethered money – quite similar to a store offering store gift cards against cash below par value. It may be a win–win situation.

Similar arrangements can be carried out with respect to mortgages and re-tirement plans that practically serve every public behavior goal deemed worthy by the legislative branch.

Let's ponder for a minute how different life would be. Much of the present complexity in the tax code will be expressed outside the code, through various tethering offers. Such offers are more flexible, some may be offered by the execu-tive branch without the burden of pushing each discount through Congress. But the main point is that of management, follow-up, and accounting. Tethered money has to meet its associated requirements *before* it is being spent, not *after the fact*.

Clearly the vision of *Taxation-by-Tethering* is not a very immediate prop-osition. Many stakeholders will have a hard time to decide if it serves their interests, or not, and some will say an automatic "no way," but technology cannot be stopped. Taxation-by-Tethering may be pioneered first by an adventurous mayor, then by a fence-climbing state, and gradually as the record proves the concept, it will spread – no doubt with major modifications compared to the broad-brush picture herein.

HEALTHCARE

The cost of healthcare is a big headache for developed, as well as undeveloped countries. In the undeveloped, the issue is infrastructure, access, education, and cost. In the developed countries, the main issue is cost. The infrastructure in the undeveloped and developing countries is being supported by international founda-tions, national initiatives, and private enterprises, and tethering the huge treasures allocated to the infrastructure will reduce waste, fraud, and abuse, and accelerate the buildup. The cost issue in developing countries is rooted in not having the patient in the loop. Handling the healthcare via negotiation between the insurers, the hospitals, the pharmaceuticals, and the individual healthcare providers allow for parochial interests to coincide into a reality of runaway cost. The Affordable Healthcare Act in the United States has not reversed this trend. Healthcare claims 7% of the US economy, and many visionaries suggested solutions involving the pa-tient in the loop. Tethered digital money could serve as a platform for any of these solutions. Insurers could prepay the patient with money that would not be spendable except for, say, the medical procedure the patient needs, as determined by a qualified doctor. The patient will then visit various clinics, holding the money in his pocket, and negotiate his best deal, with the program allowing the patient to use the money he so saves, for a related healthcare expense, for himself or his family.

Mandating the use of tracking tethered money by hospitals will allow an examiner to follow such money from minting to redemption to see who the hospital paid what, and where did the money go then.

Healthcare is engaged in a race, which is almost impossible to win. The better it is, the longer people live; but the longer they live, the greater the life-cycle healthcare cost. In the developing countries, healthcare keeps healthier, working age individuals who contribute to the economy, compensating for the investment of keeping them healthy. In developed countries, the claimants of the lion's share of healthcare cost are way past productivity age. This is getting even worse, as modern economies turn high-tech, and a smaller fraction of generally young, freshly educated people carry almost the entire production order. Tethered money is in an excellent position to be used and exploited by creative thinkers with ambition to turn things around.

GAMBLING

Looking for transactional environments, which are "hot" in more ways than one? Then look no further than gambling, lotteries, and raffles. We should carefully sidestep the moral and social aspects of games of chance, and note that states and governments officially dislike gambling so long as the operators are not them. Many states can't resist the income stream that flows from public gambling. Brick and mortar casinos have proliferated recently throughout the United States, but the online variety has not. The reason is that it is very hard for a US state to lay hands, and properly tax an elusive online casino registered in Gibraltar. So, US credit card companies (virtually all) are forewarned from taking charges on behalf of such establishments.

Tethered money could easily resolve this taxing dilemma: simply "paint" online gambling money for what it is, and as the casino (or the occasional winner) come to the mint for redemption, the mint does so at a discounted rate, where the difference goes mostly to the tax collector, and some to the service provider (the mint itself). Tethering may be designed to be quite strict so that a gambler from New York buying gambling money (digital) will have to identify himself; first, for the state of New York, to claim its share of whatever taxes they care to levy; and second, to follow-up on gambling activity. This will spot heavy gamblers that raise suspicion of some kind, and it would prevent a money launderer from claiming: "Oh, I made all this money in the casino, hit a lucky streak!"

Again, no opinion on the concept of gambling as such is being forwarded here, only a technical solution for a situation that is much worse without it.

Be it as it may, the next listed use of tethered money is completely noble.

CHARITY

In poor countries, charity is mostly touch and sweat, but in the First World, people have less time, prefer less sweat, but enjoy discretionary income more. They are happy to share some of it with the less fortunate. Only that most of us are busy with our own kind, and have little exposure to those less fortunate. Realizing this disconnect, some able planners have put up charity organizations that declare their aim to take donations and contributions from the busy affluent. These enterprises are enticing: you write the check, and we take care of the rest; spot a worthy recipient, and make some good happen.

Many fine charity organizations dedicate their efforts to noble causes of all sorts. Yet, the press is full of, what else, stories of abuse and misuse. So much cash, so many temptations! The public is shocked and gives less. The solution: tethered money, aimed and sent directly to the needy (all you need is a phone number, or an email address). The texted money can be tethered to food supply, construction company, medical health professional, etc. Some such charity money may be spread over many months; others may be anchored on some expected event or accomplishment. Tethering money allows the donor to guide his donation to the target he or she prefers, and set it to work as he or she envisions (after all it is his or her money). The sense of direct contribution is empowering, and will send the needy more of what they need. There may be many add-ons and modifications, just a matter of imagination. One such example is as follows.

Alice, generous and forthcoming, has written a check for $1000 to her favorite cause, say helping wounded war veterans, or sheltering hungry and lost cats. The cause will turn around, and pay back to Alice the sum of $500 – in digital cash. Cash tethered to the donation category, against every dollar so tethered, the bearer has contributed a dollar to a worthy (listed) cause. Alice will now challenge, say, the furniture store where she buys a comfortable chair for her living room: will you grant me a discount, say, of 15%, if I pay you with donation money? If you do, then you share with me the act of social donation. The store might build its community image by posting a sign that says that donation money will incur a 15% discount. Alice might offer her donation money when she pays for her friends in a restaurant, then it becomes known to all that Alice is generous. This simple scheme will benefit the causes participants donate to, will grant the donors nice discount in some stores, and build a nice image to stores that offer such discount. Win to all.

So many artists of all sorts find themselves in dark unlit corners – no name, no market, no pay. Their product – a painting, a sculpture, an artifact – is unique and represents a great deal of effort. The artists could showcase their wares in a dedicated website that is selling its products only against good-cause dollars: dollars that were reissued against a donation of the same amount to a worthy cause. The cause benefits from increased donation, the donors forever claim that this or that painting is original and was bought from a donor-only website, and of course, the artists will enjoy some limelight on their work.

This website one-of-a-kind sale can operate against dollars that are tethered to a certificate that asserts that these dollars were given to the bearer against good labor and community service performed for a good and recognized cause.

DEATH WISH

The business of writing a will is knottier and knottier as the estate involved is larger and larger. The language, the executor, the contenders, the law – a whole genre of literature was established over inheritance wars. Tethered money to the rescue! Major parts of a nominal will could be readily replaced with tethering the assets, and relying on the disinterested mint to carry out the wish of the departed. There are two levels: (1) buying tethered cash and (2) monetizing assets. The will writer could buy one million dollar from the mint, tethered to little Johnny upon reaching the age of 21. Johnny will be in possession of the digitized money, but will have to be old enough to redeem it, and make use of it. Sweet Nancy could be gifted $50,000 a year for the next 10 years by buying half a million digitized dollars, breaking it up to 10 coins, and marking each coin with the fitting redemption date (earning interest in the meanwhile). In a typical case the estate includes, say, a nice old home, which the will writer could digitize *per se*, and hand over a percentage of the asset in the form of a digitized claim check, which the holder can trade with, put up as collateral, etc. Digitized claim checks are readily passed around. By comparison, any change in the list of owners of a real estate is a complex public registration. The will writer could deal with a mint based in a state or country of his or her choosing to guard the will against the all so common legal hounds.

WORLD BANK

About two billion people on this planet are protected from starvation and death by the organization of international help – the World Bank, commanding respect and admiration throughout. It was only when I walked into the bank's headquarters in Washington DC that I learned about the painful inefficiency of the money flow, due to corrupt regimes and local criminals. The majority of the money intended for the least fortunate among us, ends up in Swiss bank accounts, or in similar financial havens. There is nothing more fitting for tethered money than this situation. If the World Bank would issue digital money that can be redeemed by the local construction company, the local food purveyor, the local school then it would make no sense to siphon such money to Zurich. And yes, criminals are wily and will find ways around it, but not as easy as now, not for such large sums as now.

The World Bank could do even more: hand out cheap cell phones (mobile phone towers are already virtually everywhere). The phone will be good to talk, text, and serve as wallets for digital money. Poor people anywhere would use their phone as their bank (now they sometime travel hours to the closest bank branch); they would pay from their phone (by text, or email) – now they may have to take three buses to the offices of the local utility company to pay a monthly bill; they would get paid to their phone, and tether the money to themselves – now they carry cash that tempts thieves and robbers. The World Bank could beam down a tiny amount of $10 a month, and give a whole community the credit boost that is their best bet to escape their miserable lot.

EMERGENCY MANAGEMENT

When disaster strikes, the convenience of clouds and normal electronic transactions disappears in a sudden. Millions of people are catapulted into a primitive state where most of modern amenities cease to exist. Such are mega climate occurrences, or acts of man-made mass violence and civil disruption. In those catastrophes, the only way to exercise payment is old-fashioned cash. Alas, most people in the western economies don't hoard cash in their premises; they rely on electronic means that are omnipresent on regular days, but that are defunct in time of a major disaster. Although a great many people volunteer time and resources to help their neighbors and other victims of the disaster, it is not realistic to expect the emporium owner to give away his goods or to expect a gas station operator to pump gas for free. In the event of a major community disaster, it is paramount to allow people to trade, exchange, and cooperate into bouncing back. And hence it is critical for the disaster management authority to consider tethered money for the purpose. The digital money mint will be able to prepare and store a sufficient amount of cash on hand, digital cash that is. All that cash will be tethered to a release signal by a qualified authority. This signal will be given out only after the crisis strikes. That crisis money, or emergency money, will be the fiat currency during the life of the disaster. When the crisis is over, this crisis money will be redeemable against regular money, and itself become null and void. Such tethering will allow the crisis management authority and the people involved to store the emergency money in convenient locations; so that it can be put into use with ease, as the need arises. Naturally, without access to the mint itself, the trade with digital money becomes a greater challenge. This challenge can be resolved either by battery-operated cryptographic verifiers for the validity of the money, or by the use of hybrid coin.

A desperate motorist uses his last gallon of gas to drive to the gas station in the midst of an after-storm network shutdown. The station may use a generator to pump the gas, but the motorist cannot use his credit card to pay for it. Like most of us, the motorist does not have any cash on him. A tethered money solution works as follows: the motorist uses his smartphone like a bank account, and keeps there a nice sum of money tethered to himself (like the old traveler's checks). The money is not at risk because it is replaceable, if the phone is stolen or lost. The motorist will communicate with the station's point of sale terminal, or with a seller's smartphone, using battery power and a local communication network such as NFC or Bluetooth. This communication will allow the motorist to pass his digital money to the gas station. Along with the digital money, the motorist will use a preallocated private key to certify that this money transfer is bona fide, and to identify himself as the rightful owner of the passed dollars. The private key will certify the identity of the motorist. It would be technically possible for the motorist to fake digital currency and pass it on, but this fraud will eventually be flashed out when the network is reestablished. When this happens, it constitutes a proven crime and the identity of the criminal is known. The police will prosecute, and the various institutions that issue credibility certificates and credit rating scores will slap this fraudster with a public profile that will reflect his criminal activity. This will be enough to prevent virtually everyone from passing fake money. The tiny fraction of remaining thieves will be readily covered with insurance. This solution exploits the fact that local communication and cryptographic calculations can be carried out in a network shutdown, using just battery power.

The hybrid coins solution to make payments in a network shutdown is based on the pre-crisis credibility buildup of these coins. The coin is physical, with a visual indication of "virginity" – never being busted open. Past experience shows that such a coin (plastic or metal), when cracked open, always included a microSD or similar bit storage that could be readily uploaded to one's computer, and be honored by the mint. Therefore, the gas station operator will be glad to accept them at par value.

INSURANCE

"Superstorm Sandy" moved fast and hard (2012), devastating stretches of crowded neighborhoods throughout the New York and New Jersey coast lines. AIG, the world largest insurer, was on the spot for compensating the tens of thousands whose home was damaged. The political pressure to cut the checks and move on was relentless. When agents inspected the area a few months later, they learned to their dismay that many recipients of the checks that averaged at around $50,000 each used only a fraction of it, to barely rebuild their home, and applied the balance to buy a fancy car or a boat. The rebuilt houses were so flimsy that a tiny storm will redestroy them. In order to receive their rebuilding checks, the insured had to commit to using the funds to reconstruct the damaged structure in a robust fashion, to minimize the chance that AIG will have to pay for another rebuilding. The clear violation of the pay-off agreement would have likely won thousands of court victories to AIG. But as AIG Chief Technology Officer intimated to me: yes, we could have hired a brigade of lawyers, but, no, we won't fall into this trap. Had AIG been cutting tethered checks, redeemable only by home contractors, their problem would have never arisen.

TRUST TRAP

When the United States safeguarded gold belonging, say, to the French government, they would invite a French representative to the vault at Ft. Knox to see his shinny bricks. But when Bernie Madoff did the same for Elie Wiesel and countless others, he simply showed them a neat, official looking statement certifying their assets in glowing numbers. Madoff victims are so used to trust, they didn't think twice about it. When we get our monthly bank statement, do we try to make a payment out of each account to verify the printout? This is a fertile ground for "fifty shades of fraud": from slight misrepresentation by an otherwise respected financial institution to a sheer Madoff class theft. Indeed, it is hard to follow on all the money movements exercised by a trusted agent. Your money chases opportunities, is recast, divided, combined – with some very risky gaps in between, how are you to know. Insurance companies declare that they invest only in low-risk avenues so they are ready to pay off their clients when called upon. But will you know whether they succumbed to an attractive scheme with a risk level beyond comfort?

Suppose now that digitized money technology is expanding to digitize precious metals, oil wells, stocks, real estate, etc. Once so these assets are subject to tethering just as the old greenback is. For you as a trusting client this means that you could insure that the money and asset you hand over in trust to a financial wizard will be restricted to be exchanged, divided, manipulated, etc., only among assets that submit to the same low-risk quality. In other words, your agent, having control of your money, would be able only to use it to buy, say, gold, or blue chip stocks that are themselves digitized and also tethered with the same grade of risk.

It is the beauty of tethering. You can't tether a brick of gold. The brick goes anywhere betrays not its origin. (How many gold bricks are traded today, their gold having been plucked from mouths of dead Jews piled up in the gas chambers of Auschwitz?) But you can readily tether a digital claim check for that gold to bear witness to its origin, and to limit its use only to buy properly tethered assets.

TETHERED TRADE

The Internet condensed the people on this planet into cyber neighbors, where each of our seven billion counts, can trade with anyone else. When strangers trade, they face a well-expected trust problem. So often the buyer sends the money, and the merchandise does not arrive, or vice versa, the seller sends the merchandise, and does not get paid. When the traders are a world apart, they have no practical way to sue each other, not to speak of the burden and the cost of international legal action. Tethering will come in handy. The buyer will send the money to the seller, tethered to the eventual nod from him that the merchandise arrived in good order. The seller receiving the tethered money will verify with the mint that the money is good, and is payable. He will then send the merchandise and wait for the buyer to signal OK to the mint for it to release the money to the seller's account. If the buyer refuses to send the "good-to-pay" signal, then the traders will move on to a preagreed-upon procedure, perhaps arbitration. But such procedure happens when the money of the transaction is in limbo – held by the mint, and is at the disposal of neither the buyer nor the seller. This means that both traders have a strong incentive to resolve the disagreement.

Tethered trade may also serve as a viable alternative to contract work. In many instances, the customer pays, say, a third before the work starts, a third when half is done, and a third when the work is done. This arrangement still allows each trader to behave dishonestly for one third of the sum. Tethering as above will eliminate that.

Tethering may be used to implement any other trade arrangements. A buyer may offer a bonus if the seller finishes a product earlier. The buyer will prepare two tethered coins, one for the regular price tethered toward a proof of delivery submitted by the carrier and another coin tethered to the seller and subject to the condition that the delivery date as indicated by the carrier, is earlier than a set date. Otherwise, the coin reverts to the buyer. The seller is thereby assured that the bonus money is payable.

TETHERING TRADE

Tethering may be viewed as a liability levied on the possessor of the tethered money. This liability needs to be paid in order to untether the money. Alice, then, could sell her tethered coin to Bob against the nominal value of the coin minus a discount that will represent the measure of the tethered liability. For example, Alice got hold of a coin for the sum of $1000, tethered to residents of Rockville, Maryland. Alice could travel to Rockville and spend the $1000 there, where merchants have strong incentives to accept it (say a tax discount). Albeit, Alice lives too far from the town, so she sells the coin to Bob, a Rockville resident, for $925 – untethered. Bob will easily spend the money in his neighborhood. Some form of charity will tether a contribution to the claimant engaging in 25 hours of community service. Once the service is certified, the money is released. Alice would sell a $1000 coin to Bob for $500 because Bob will have to labor 25 hours for it. Of course, many tethers are not transferrable, but those that are can evolve into a busy market.

RETETHERING

A tethered coin may be retethered. Alice holds a coin tethered to be redeemed only by the *Letters Book Store*. She can further tether that coin to be good only within 6 months from now, and then hand it over to Bob. Bob, in turn, could re-tether again, and exchange this coin by another with same denomination with a third requirement: it is good only for nonfiction books. Bob then hands over the coin to Carla. For Carla to redeem the coin, she needs to prove to the mint that she used it in the *Letters Book Store* within 6 months, and that she bought a non-fiction book. Alice and Bob can readily retether an already tethered coin, but they cannot untether it without fulfilling the tethering requirement. Whether Alice can untether a coin she tethered is a matter of agreement between Alice and the mint.

Retethering may involve coin exchange. Alice, holding a tethered coin X, will ask the mint to exchange it against a new coin of equal value, Y, where Y is tethered to the X-tethering along with new tethering ordered by Alice. It will have the same effect as adding the new tethering to coin X.

Retethering is useful also in a project environment where successive managers at lower levels add tethering to manage their turf. Retethering can also be applied using surrogate mints and subcontracted tethering.

PERSONAL PAYMENT AND PRIVACY

The power to tether money is strongly pronounced upon us as individuals. The strongest impact is in the war against government prying into individual conduct. Today, most of us use electronic transactions to shop online and in face-to-face occasions. This commonplace habit develops massive amount of data with which anyone with access to this data (the service provider, the government, those who buy the data, and those who steal it), can carefully and intrusively profile us all. Millions of law-abiding citizens are exposed as per their taste in books, food, clothes, vacations, and even more intimate and personal matters for which most of us would insist on privacy. Digital money *per se* will be the most important weapon in this privacy campaign. That is because it works like cash. The value of the transaction is verified regardless of the identity of the payer. Not to speak about the payer not exposing any hackable account.

The single most critical problem for straight payment of digital money is that the smartphone that stores our money may be lost or stolen, and in that case it is like losing one's wallet – the thief takes away the money. Enters tethering: a personal user will tether the bulk of his money to himself. Such money will be useable and redeemable only by the person who originally bought those digital coins in the first place. It will work like an electronic version of the familiar concept of travelers' checks. Alice will load her phone with $3000, $2800 of it is tethered to herself as the only redeemer, and the balance of $200 is left untethered. Now when shopping, Alice can spend up to $200 with the equivalence of cash, and when she spends it all, she will untether another chunk of $200, leaving the balance of $2600 securely tethered to her name. All this tethering and untethering is carried out by software on Alice's phone. One could ask how would the mint verify Alice's identity? This is a valid and proper question, but a separate one. Identity verification is a well-known subject with an array of solutions trading cost, security, and convenience. Alice will be able to select the one most fitting her needs.

Tethering will allow individuals to send money to a relative or a friend and limit its use to a well-defined purpose, over a well-defined window of time, as well as other terms. This in-family payment tethering is likely to be used by parents sending money to a son or daughter in college, limiting the use of the money to books and office supplies.

COMMUNITY BOOTSTRAPPING

Tethered money may be used by a community as a means to encourage mutual business and community prosperity. Tethering may be used to distinguish members of a community by designating them as the only ones qualified to redeem certain coins. This will have the net effect of private money. Much as countries enhance their economic status by trading with their own currency, and having only few exchange points with other currencies, so it is on a smaller, community scale: trading with a "private currency" has its privileges. The community of reference may be a village, a town, a society, or an association of some sort, large, small, or in between.

Let me use a personal example. The city of Rockville, Maryland, is replete with residents who work in near-by Washington DC, or across the river in Virginia. A lot of merchandise that could have been bought in Rockville and boost the local economy is actually being purchased outside the city limits. Now suppose the mayor of Rockville and the city council engage a prevailing digital mint to issue money tethered for redemption only by city residents. The city will announce a community enhancement campaign designed to attract Rockville residents to direct more of their business to the community. They declare that (1) any purchase made with tethered Rockville money (redeemable by Rockville residents only) will be charged only 3% sales tax, instead of the normal 5%; and (2) any merchant accepting Rockville tethered money will count only 85% of the revenue for the purpose of computing city income tax. Of course, the city may come up with different incentives (weaker or stronger, chasing the optimal), but the principle is to offer financial incentives for city merchants. This will motivate the merchants to offer discount against Rockville-tethered dollars, which, in turn, will motivate Rockville residents to exchange untethered dollars and buy tethered dollars. Some residents will accumulate Rockville dollars because of the incentive, and will be bound to spend them in the city itself, which they might have done anyway. Residents might adapt and buy gas in town, rather than on their way someplace far; and will buy their groceries close to home, rather than where it is convenient during lunch time. The net result will be more city business. This will result in more money collected from taxes, which, when incentives are carefully chosen, should well compensate the loss of money due to these incentives. Cities across the map could do the same, encouraging community spirit.

BURN PAY

Many payments are conducted without a payee receiving the money. The money simply "burns away" against some service. The service provider received his money when the user bought the burning money. A parking meter is a common example. A motorist will buy a digital coin that is cryptographically tethered to a specific "burning" device, namely, it cannot be redeemed anywhere, except that it can be provided to that specific device in which the money is "burned" away. The device is issued by the city, and when activated it starts burning the money attached to it (likely via a physical device). The burning continues until the money source is pulled away. The burning may correspond to time usage handled with a built-in clock and firmware programming, to compute the fare based on time of the day, and whatever other factors. The tethering is important to insure that the burnt money, when it was bought, was credited to the service provider. Burn-pay tethering may be used for utility payments, (power, gas, steam), use of copiers, printers, washing machines, etc.

PAY-AS-YOU-GO

Burn pay is one option for real-time payment (pay-as-you-go). A full transaction cycle is another option, namely, the burnt money is routed to the payee. The advantage to the payer is that he or she can buy the digital money generically, as opposed to buying it from the service provider. Closing the loop may happen wirelessly.

Utility companies all over the world have a big issue with payment delinquency. Invoices and warnings don't work very well. Cutting off supply is not a viable option, socially and politically because the afflicted are often the miserable bottom of society. Pay-as-you-go is a universal solution! Power consumers will have to use a digital money stick, latching it into a device at home. When money bits are available to be aired to the utility company, then the power is on again. The government could help the needy by allocating for them utility sticks at a planned monthly rate. These sticks will be tethered to be used only for the grid, and perhaps even restricted to a particular user. For sure such a tethered money stick voids the need for invoices, collection tactics, lawsuits, etc. And once payment is secured there will be more offering the same service.

Pay-as-you-go may be used by a car passing through a toll road, sending money bits to the transportation authority. In presenting this option to safety-minded people, the following scenario came up, and left goose bumps on more than one attendee: "Modern cars, the argument went, know the allowed speed on the stretch where they zoom by. The car certainly knows its own speed". We were slow to realize where the argument led: "... so why not mandate an algorithm that would compute speed penalty that accumulates from the instant when the car exceeds the allowed speed limit, until it goes below that limit, and at any moment the add-on penalty will be proportional to the gap between the allowed speed and the present speed." The climbing dollar figures will show prominently on the dashboard: these will be sums that are paid out as the speed progresses – not an invoice, not a warning, but money evaporating. The psychological impact will work sooner or later, and the speed will come down, as the driver is hissing some unprintable exclamations.

Equally imaginative is the following use. Power companies register great savings if the demand for electricity stays uniform throughout the day. Alas, when a heat wave visits the city, all kick up their air-conditioning units, creating costly demand peaks. The power company then will try to get people to use, say, their washing machines in off-peak hours to flatten the consumption as much as possible. Since such choice behavior saves money to the power supply company, they might as well share these savings with the well-behaving consumers, to motivate them to continue. Some utilities indeed add a rebate line on their monthly statement – which nobody reads. With digital money at hand, the utility company will text to the well-behaving consumer a real-time "thank you" note for his consideration – instant gratification. The happy consumer will order a pizza and celebrate the day with his family. Such rebate money carries with it a "green value" – it reflects money that helps the environment. It would be so tethered, allowing the consumer to present his green bills to, say, a restaurant that brags: "we offer a 5% discount to green money!"

THE NEW ELECTRICITY MARKET

Whether we are running out of oil or are just chocked on exhaust gases from fired coal plants – the trend is toward renewables, toward clean energy: solar, wind – and the configuration is one of plentiful of sellers of energy – not just your neighborhood monopoly. Alice has a big house and a big yard, and she uses her area to lay out solar panels; so many of them, that she has electricity to sell to her neighbor, Bob. A transfer grid is necessary, yes, but what about the administration: the invoicing, the payment monitoring, the dispute resolution, collection, etc.? Not worth the trouble, it seems. But it is worth the trouble because the same line where power flows from Alice to Bob will serve for Bob's money to flow back to Alice – real time, as the power is consumed.

And if Alice has a restaurant, she could offer a charging service for Bob's electrical car, operating while Bob is consuming his food. Alice could execute the transaction as a normal credit card payment and subject it to the settlement, resolution, and to a potential dispute that plagues that kind of credit card transactions. Instead, the patrons who parked their electrical cars for charging have also installed a USB stick with digital money, and the money flows in the counter direction. When the power gear is disconnected, the entire deal, payment and all is done with.

NANOPAYMENTS

Technology has created a new market for computing resources. As the Internet becomes more efficient, and as computing devices proliferate, there arises the opportunity to divide large computational tasks to a large assembly of relatively small computational activities, then distribute these activities among the myriad of connected computing machines that stand idle for long stretches of time. Today taskmasters of this practice, usually "steal" computing power from unsuspecting computer owners. But as this practice matures, computer owners will demand to be paid for dedicating their computer to an alien taskmaster. Tethered money, denominated to very low denominations (nanopayments), if so desired, may be attached as a trailer to task-definition input string as it is sent to an idle computer. The computer will figure out the required computational task, slice off the nanopayment string, and forward its output string to be sent to the client that requested the computational task. A computer "for sale" that serves to compute many tasks for many clients will add up the tethered money strings to be redeemed at the mint by the end of the day.

ACCESS VERSUS USE

In many fields, service contracts are structured around "access" as opposed to "actual use." Most of us have signed up with a cable service that gives us access to many channels we never watch – but pay for them anyway. Hotel service includes access to the pool, the gym, and the business center. Many guests use neither, but pay the same as others who use these facilities for hours. Same with subscription to a news magazine we check out occasionally. Such access contracts are easier to manage, but are inherently unfair: the low-intensity user subsidized his high-intensity counterpart. Efficient frictionless nanotransactions enable a just pay-per-use configuration.

The difference that digital money makes is in the accounting surrounding the payment. How many of us would wish to review a monthly statement from the cable company detailing which channel we watched for how many minutes, at what rate per minute? And if we see a problem in the statement, how will we settle it, how can we prove what we watched, or did not watch, 3 weeks ago? With pay-as-you-go, pay-exactly-per-use, and pay-and-forget all these issues melt away.

Today, online publishers wrestle with monetization. Most of their readers are occasional consumers who balk at a yearly subscription to a magazine they infrequently check out. Alas, to charge what is known as "micropayment" (say, a quarter per page) is infeasible, owing to the transactional overhead of any payment card deal. Desperate, publishers pollute their contents with cheap "come-ons" advertisement, with dubious utility to the advertisers, but generating indisputable resentment by their readers. Digital money with its at-will resolution, and trust oriented cryptographic protocols will allow even a pay-per-word, if deemed helpful. And what's more, the reader will pay with ecash without identifying himself, namely, without having his reading habits logged in a massive database in Nevada.

Once we get used to this modality then all sorts of transactions that are now inherently "access" based, as opposed to "use" based, will turn around. For example, access to the Internet is normally through subscription to an access provider. We pay the same whether we browse all day long, or not even turn the computer on. The low-level users subsidize the high-level users. Some beer buddies told me, half-jokingly, that they watch as many downstream movies as they can, whether they like it or not, in order to reduce the cost per movie, as they pay for access. Imagine now a situation in which every time you turn on a computing device, wishing to hook to the information highway, you first announce it and ask for bids from the prevailing connectivity vendors. They compete with prices that reflect their available bit rate at the moment, at the place, and also reflect how busy they are. Your computer will choose the most advantageous bid and start a session. The deal will close when the session is over. The next time, another bidding war and a different selection. There are standard pricing models that duly assure us that prices will drop considerably through this ad-hoc bidding game, and even Internet hook-up companies will benefit because they will have means to attract consumers in slow time (offer good prices), and protect themselves from being chocked (via high quotes). Again, it all works because digital money payment will counterflow real time – no after-fact accounting, no invoicing, etc. The same solution will work for WiFi. Instead of begging for free access from a local WiFi station, users could offer to pay-per-use time.

The pay per use offers another critical advantage: privacy. Today my Internet provider knows exactly how I behave online. After all, they are enabling this behavior. They know it even if I use an "incognito" browser, and so much of who I am, and what I do, what I care about, is captured in my online behavior! If I no longer subscribe to Verizon, as I do now, and I buy ad-hoc connection sessions, once from Verizon, next from AT&T, etc., then neither Verizon, nor AT&T have this complete wall-to-wall picture of my daily behavior. It is like the difference between using Uber to move about Manhattan, as opposed to a random cab. Uber knows every trip I make, however, embarrassing. By comparison, hailing a taxi each ride *per se* secures my privacy, especially if I pay cash, then nobody has the total picture of my city behavior.

NAPSTER REVIVED

It was a flash and a sizzle like never before in the music industry, a tech creature called Napster upset the apple cart, and effected lightning fast distribution of songs – free of charge! Eventually, it was the "free of charge" attribute of Napster that influenced the Supreme Court of the United States to shut it down. Yet, its peer-to-peer distribution mode is so technologically supreme that it was just a matter of time before one comes up with a way to use this distribution mode without robbing the rights of owners.

Tethered micropayment is that technology. Alice uses Napster, or an equivalent "middle-man," to realize that Bob has her favorite song on his computer. She then propositions Bob to sell her the song. Bob will set up a price. If his price would be too high, Alice will keep shopping for a better price, so Bob will not be greedy, and set his price to $0.40. Alice will agree, and forthwith execute a protocol in which Bob downloads the song to her, while she uploads the digital money (40 cents) to him. By the end of the day, Bob will collect all the digital money he got from selling the popular song to Alice and others, and approach the digital mint with a demand to redeem it. Examining Bob's digital coins, the mint readily realizes the coins for what they are and activates the proper protocol. The mint redeems to Bob only 30 cents for the song he sold Alice. The balance, of 10 cents, is cut into 8 cents that are credited to the rights' owner for this song, and 2 cents that the digital mint collects for this service (or similar numbers, of course). It does not take much imagination to see this trade evolving so that the long paws of the tax collector reach out to this effective pay-as-you-go modality. By contrast to the original Napster, the new version makes everyone happy, except perhaps the old music store in the mall.

LOYALTY PROGRAMS

The majority of US purchases are carried out on a competitive and repetitive basis. Items people buy, they often buy again. The seller they bought it from may be readily replaced by its competitor. This state of affairs prompts merchants to spur up loyalty programs – means to keep their customers buying from them.

The more an item is a commodity, the more its price counts, and hence merchants compete through price discounts. It was quite long ago when merchants realized that the discount or pay-back they offer to their customer does not have to be untethered money – money the customer is free to use as he or she sees fit. That discount may be *tethered* to subsequent purchases from the same merchant.

What a simple idea: practice price competition by offering discounts comprising tethered money. The customer then will have the choice: either to lose that money or to use it by buying from the same source. Now, most buyers "fall into a groove" – they buy for the same amount from the very same merchant – a matter of habit. And hence they don't suffer from the subtle replacement of untethered money with tethered funds.

The merchants tried and loved it. And a lot of creative juices have flown into this "racket." Programs have been devised to increase consumption by augmenting the tethering world into a threshold basis – the consumer gets nothing until he or she exceeds a preset threshold. So many consumers buy more than they need to reach that threshold.

Merchants found that it pays off to associate various levels of purchasing with some prestige of belonging to a club that exudes an air of privilege; however, baseless. Today, we witness a rich variety of loyalty programs ranging from the coalition concept where two or more merchants share discount applicability, to vanity rich perks to the few who qualify.

Whatever the terms, a tethered digital money mint will be an ideal environment to execute these payments. The reason is that the digital money mint offers a standard efficient structure to tether money to any and all conditions that can be spelled out as an algorithm. Not only is the tethered digital mint standardized and, as such, much more efficient than the standalone instances of tethered money, but also it associates the tethering with the money itself. What is the big advantage here? The mint, the central authority for the loyalty program does not have to manage a detailed account status for all its customers. The customers themselves, on their computing devices will keep track of all the loyalty funds they have, and dedicated software, referencing any pending purchase, lines up the discount money logically (starting with the ones with a shorter expiration date).

Today, my United air-miles are managed by a United database. I need to talk to a person to claim a free flight or to transfer the miles to someone else. Using tethered money technology, United will mint and issue to me tethered money that is only good to pay for a United flight under whatever restrictions and conditions they have contrived for me. Once this tethered money bill is issued to me, all that United has to do is to keep a copy of this coin, but it would no longer need to maintain my account where it manages all the air miles I accumulate. The next time I would book a flight my own phone would forward applicable tethered money as part or whole of the payment, and all that United will have to check is that the coin was actually issued by it, and was not redeemed before.

I have lodged at the Hilton many a time, and the Hilton chain manages my "points" and "privileges," keeping track of when I am eligible for some freebie. The Hilton database has nothing to do with my United air-miles accounting database and should United and Hilton decide to cross-honor each other's reward points, they will face quite a management burden. However, if both loyalty programs fit into the same die-cast of tethered money, then creating a coalition between the two would be a simple software instruction, and the same for any third party joining into a threesome coalition.

The greater impact of the standardized tethered money paradigm is in allowing merchants to offer their customers a loyalty program without incurring the heavy burden of paying for a dedicated setup. A willing merchant will sign on at the tethered money mint website, spell out its terms, and the mint will issue to it the tethered money for distribution among its customers – much easier, much cheaper. With tethered money small merchants can level the playing field and offer reward points and loyalty programs like the "big boys." The march of personal gadgetry allows for unprecedented dynamics and creativity in loyalty programs. Merchants today identify their customer by his smartphone. The phone tells them where the customer is located, and how far from their store. The merchant also knows the purchasing habit of the customers, partly from their own record, and partly from fishing the Web and through social media. And then sophisticated algorithms offer "deals" and "discounts." Some of these offers have a lifetime of 2 hours or less. It is nearly impossible for a merchant to prevail in this regimen of stiff dynamic discounts without using a robust efficient mechanism to manage, express, and redeem its coupons and reward points, and purchase certificates. The standardized tethered money platform will enable this critical efficiency.

Much as Google's innovative idea of "AdWords" lowered the threshold for merchants to advertise their goods, so should the standardized loyalty program draw in the mom-and-pop stores, and make commerce more fair and more competitive.

Many loyalty programs today exploit a very powerful and interesting concept: *unpaid-for coupons*. A merchant will advertise in a local paper, and the advertisement will feature a label with a number, saying, for instance, $3.00 discount coupon for your next pizza. Let's say that the local paper has 100,000 copies printed weekly. This computes to $300,000 worth of discount. Normally, only a handful of diners cut the coupon and hand it over as a $3.00 equivalent. In this setting, the merchant does not pay the $300,000 up front – the coupons are "dead money" that springs into life when a diner hands it over while paying for a pizza (the particular type of pizza, and before the coupon expires).

How can such "dead money" be implemented within the tethered money platform?

The tethered money platform offers two mechanisms to handle this case. One is *tethered money activation* and the other is *coin imaging*.

Activation works as follows: a merchant plans to email tethered money to its customers. It knows from experience that, say, 10% of these money bills are exercised in its stores, so he offers to pay the mint 10% of the total value of these digital money bills. The mint prepares the coins for the merchant, but marks them all as "inactive" or as "undetermined," and then allows for redemption up to the count that was paid for, and allows for the rest as soon as the merchant pays up. This solution is important in case of coalition rewards where the emailed funds may be redeemed in any of several coalition members.

Imaging works as follows: a merchant requests the mint to mint coin images at various indicated denominations and various counts. All images, no money, so the merchant does not have to pay for the coins – they only look like coins, but they are not coins. The merchant will be asked to pay for the mint service, but not as per the values of the coin images. The merchant will then distribute the coin images to customers or to prospective customers. For the customer, the coin image that reads, say, $25, is worth $25, and so the customer brings the coin image to the merchant and claims its worth. Two options may be applicable now. One where the merchant's computer has a copy of the distributed images and it manages them, and the other where the merchant will pass the $25 coin image to the mint for approval. The mint simply checks if the submitted coin image is a coin image that was minted by the mint, and not a fabrication, and then it checks if the same coin image was not submitted for redemption earlier. If the $25 coin image passes both tests, then it communicates this fact to the merchant. The merchant charges that customer $25 less.

One would readily conclude that both activation and coin imaging are valid solutions to account for the "dead money" practice in loyalty currency.

In summary, the universal framework of tethered digital money offers a range of advantages over the prevailing private and noncommunicative solutions for the world of loyalty programs.

The above-mentioned concepts of "activation" and "coin imaging" are further elaborated in subsequent sections.

Activation

Tethered digital money comes with a unique feature of several uses: *activation*. Every minted coin may be associated with an "active/inactive" tag. Active means it's good to trade with; inactive implies not tradable. This so-called activation tag may be applied to a whole class of coins, and even to the mint as a whole. That tag may also be minted as a "qtag" or as "undetermined" in which case the activation status of the coin is not determined on the coin itself but must be specified in the mint management data. This will allow the mint to wholesale deactivate an entire class of coins, and then class reactivate them. The mint activation tag will override the coin tag.

This tag may be used to quickly freeze transactions that became suspect, and then unfreeze them, if and when the suspicion proves to be unwarranted. It may be used by loyalty programs to freeze off loyalty currency coins, either permanently or as per certain periods. And it may be used for various applications where coins and money are prepared for a certain purpose and it is activated only when needed. This will reduce motivation to steal such money while it is still worthless. Preparing money, perhaps hybrid coins, to distribute to a population when recovering from a large area disaster may also be a proper application of the activation option.

Imaging

An image of a coin is a data entity that looks like a coin, may have all the features of a coin, including an indication of value, but it carries no value. It is not a coin; it is nonredeemable. The use of a coin image may be applicable for simulation of trade, and as a vehicle to carry coin or payment information for a related transaction. The first can be used in games, modeling exercises, running economic simulators, and for entertainment and educational purposes. The latter may be used to allow tethered money to be used in the credit market.

A coin image is so indicated by an image tag that should prevent any confusion between it and a real coin. A coin image is not a deactivated coin. The latter is a real coin for which redemption is blocked, but for which redemption can be unblocked at any instance. By contrast, a coin image cannot become a coin, it is only an information vehicle that flows around like coins, but has no value and cannot be marked as value, as money.

CREDIT

For the first half of the twentieth century, consumers who needed credit applied for a loan, and started to pay interest on it from day one, although they deposited the money with the bank until such time they actually needed it. At the same time businesses were issued a line of credit, which they used when called for. It was not a big leap for Bank of America, in 1958, to offer a similar deal to consumers via a payment card. It was not very well organized, credit worthiness was not thoroughly checked, but the program survived, and in the mid-1960s, it even took off, first in California, then throughout the States. Led by a creative mind, Dee Hock, the renamed Visa organization built a configurational marvel where the clients, the members, the governors, and the governed were one and the same. Naming this new creature "Chaord" – a synthesis between chaos and order, Mr Hock went through ups and downs until Visa came to dominate the payment landscape worldwide. By now, Visa is a mushrooming complexity where issuer banks and acquirer banks follow ever more complicated protocols, adjusting for a growing size, faster speed, piling up regulations, and the ever-looming threat of cyber attacks. Today, Visa is a treading giant. Together with its next in size, MasterCard, it moves and exchanges more than $5 trillion annually, dominating the industry, choking all competition, and squeezing its dependent merchants with steep service fees.

This is a remarkable record. When Visa started, typewriters were in vogue. Although so many big names of the precomputer era failed and vanished under the colossal sea change of the combined computing-communication technology, Visa proved itself a survivor, adapting, triumphing throughout. Visa accommodated the personal computer, the screeching modem-based communication, and the high-speed Internet. And now it faces digital currency: start-up, novice, controversial.

What was the big shout of the early Visa? Trust, the brand. The idea was to use a name everyone heard of, trusted, and respected. Merchants accepted cash and checks, why should they release their merchandise for plastic? What if they don't get paid? After all, the customer just scribbled his signature on a piece of paper. Apprehension dominated, but Dee Hock was diligent, creative, and unyielding. He knew that he needed to get a few merchants in each local market, then the others will join, not to lose business. The little window sticker with the Visa emblem became a merchant's survival must. Banks throughout the country so realized, and gave up competing individually. More and more joined this remarkable membership organization, leading it to dominance.

The organizational nightmare faced by Dee was the fact that banks issued cards to close-by neighbors, but those neighbors would travel afar, where they expected their card to be honored. The web of issuers and acquirers is where the action is, where the power resides.

Now let's reexamine these tenets. How important is a brand name? In the twentieth century, merchants relied on Visa promise to make the merchant whole in case of fraud. But today merchants release their merchandise not before the issuer bank OKs the purchase. So the name on the card could be Lisa, not Visa, because the brand name had no more role to play.

The second observation is even more powerful. The competition over good borrowers sent issuers outside their neighborhood. A new industry emerged: credit reporting firms. Bank increasingly relied on one's credit score for risk assessment and issuance decisions.

Let's wrap our mind around these two observations, and let's do so with digital money in mind. Where does it lead us? We should clearly realize that the big expensive brand name is no longer needed. If Alice shows some digital sequence to a merchant, and on account of this bit string the merchant is paid the purchase price – digitally on the spot, no delay – then why should the merchant care what is the name on Alice's card? Oh, yes, she does not even have a card (not even old faithful EMV), Alice has a phone. And the merchant bears no risk. Neither does the mint because it does not pay the merchant before it gets paid by the issuer bank – the lender.

And lo and behold, where did the network go? It's not needed anymore. In the past, the banks collectively and the network shared risk and responsibility. In the new regimen, risk is assumed only by the lender. And because of that, the lender may rely on the national credit report (in the United States, not so else-where), and on local scouts who would spot good risks in their neighborhoods. The lender will contract local people/firms with good standing in the commu-nity, and task them to scout for good risk borrowers.

The technical aspects are secondary, but here is one: the credit extension is carried out with a coin image, as discussed earlier, not a coin *per se*. A coin image looks like a coin, has a nominal value, splits like a coin, and passes like a coin, but it is not a coin. It is not even a deactivated coin; it is simply an infor-mation bearer. The lender will order from the mint a coin image string bearing the sum of, say, $1,000,000. The lender will allocate a coin image denominated for $2500 to Alice and $1000 to Bob. Alice would shop for a large-screen TV, priced for $800, and decide to use her credit. She will use her phone to send to the merchant a $800 split of her $2500 coin image (remember: coin images split like coins). The merchant reading the header on the bit string will realize this is a coin image, read the identification of the bit mint, and dispatches the coin im-age over. The mint will check that the bit string is bona fide, and that the image was not used before, and if Ok, then the mint will communicate the details to the lender. The lender will verify the data on its part, and will expedite to the mint $800 – this time it is real money, a bona fide digital coin, issued perhaps (but not necessarily) by the same mint. No sooner has the mint received the lender's pay, than it will rush that money to the merchant, who will release the wide-screen TV to Alice. The deal is done except that the lender will need, in due course, to get paid by Alice.

These newly emerging payment configurations that bypass the formerly one-route-fits-all network-dominated option, will likely lead to regulatory eas-ing, which might bring nonbank entities into the credit market. Come to think about it, an employer is in a much better position to assess credit worthiness. The local city too, it can shut the water to nonpayers. Digital money credit is a teeming topic ready for imagination blessed entrepreneurs to dive in, and take us over to promising well-leveraged territory.

THE BANKING PARADOX

Nominally, one can either use her money in business or pleasure or, alternatively, put the money in the bank as an investment. She will then collect interest or watch her stock appreciate. What is not possible today is to do both simultaneously. The tethered digital money paradigm miraculously allows one to use money in payment, and collect interest on the same, or alternatively gamble on stock with the same funds. Alice may buy, say, a $1000 coin from the mint, and direct the mint to deposit the money in an interest bearing account. If the annual interest, say, is 4% (one has to use long-term memory to regard this figure as real ...) then if Alice holds on to her digital coin for 1 year she will redeem her coin against $1040. (In practice, it will be less because the mint will likely charge a service fee or take a slice from the accumulated interest). However, Alice does not have to hold the digital coin in her phone, she can use it to pay Bob, and Bob may pass the money on to Carla. Carla, say, redeems the coin exactly a year after its purchase. Carla then gets $1000 but Alice is credited with $40 – the interest accumulated over a year. The bank would not care that Alice used the digital coin in payment. It cares only about the time between deposit and withdrawal. Alice could give the $1000 digital coin to Bob as an installment pay and tether it to be redeemed only 6 months from now. Bob can verify that the coin is good, and stands for $1000, so he is not subject to the risk of Alice not coming through with her payment, but Alice earns the interest for these 6 months as if she deposited the money in the bank and paid Bob only 6 months ahead. This notion of *interest-bearing working capital* will generally ease the pain of the float associated with prepaid accounts. Traders could take out large sums of money, tethered to themselves as the sole authorized redeemers (hence, these funds are very secure), and regularly convert small amounts to untethered money (lost if stolen). If they earn the prevailing interest on this large sum, they keep tethered on their phone, then these traders enjoy the ready flexibility of cash on hand while earning interest on the same as if it were deposited unused in the bank. Interest-bearing digital coins will be of great service for large projects with large sums of money managed through tethering.

Alice could buy a digital coin denominated in stock, and pay the coin as an installment pay to Bob, agreeing with Bob to jointly bet on the price of the stock. Like in the former example, Alice is scheduled to make a $1000 payment to Bob, 6 months from now. She will direct the mint to buy 100 shares of a stock worth $10 a share, such that the redeemer of the coin will be handed back the 100 shares whatever their value at the time of the redemption. She will then agree with Bob that they share the profit and the loss 50:50. So, if 6 months ahead when the coin satisfied its redemption time restriction, Bob redeems it, at $8.00 a share, then Alice will owe him $100 for her part in the loss of $200. In the case where the share will sell at $11.00, 6 months from now, then Bob will owe Alice $50, her part in the appreciation of the stock. Of course, Alice and Bob can cut any deal they wish, the mint is not involved. It simply returns the stock upon redemption of the coin.

Digital coins are expected to become the norm, and more and more traders will redeem coins paid to them against another digital coin that they would tether to their desires, as opposed to getting a check back, or a deposit into their old-fashioned bank account. The result will be that the original deposit that purchased the first coin in the sequence will stay alive longer and longer before it is turned back to the form of money with which the original coin was paid. This, in turn, implies that interest money will become a more serious factor on account of longer intervals between deposit and withdrawal. But the more this trend continues, the lower the interest will become because the banks that hold the deposits will find fewer and fewer borrowers for that money – most borrowers will go digital.

IN THE HANDS OF OUR ADVERSARIES

A good chess player keeps himself busy thinking his opponent's moves, as much as she thinks of her own. Tethered money is a powerful technology that can serve our adversaries, and against which we need to be prepared. Any confederacy of tax evaders will be able to establish a mint and trade with tethered money internally. This confederacy will need only one well-concealed exchange point with the fiat currency. To join this confederacy, a newcomer will exchange, say, his dollars against the confederacy currency, and use the latter to trade with other confederates. All that internal trade is invisible to the Internal Revenue Service, and no taxes are paid. Members can, at will, sell their confederate currency against dollars. It is easy to see how such a hidden mint will serve as a very effective route for the massive amount of money that desperately is looking now for laundering routes, especially after the US Federal government applied heavy pressure on tax havens around the world.

Tax evasion is one threat. More serious than that is the funding of criminal and terrorism enterprise where tethered money may replace the Hawala – the informal untraceable money transfers that served terrorists for years. Digital currency hides well in the ocean of crypto flow on the Internet. Money and value may be exchanged and remain undiscovered.

INTERNATIONAL SCOPE

Two mutually not-so-friendly countries live in mutual separation. One country has extra bolts with no nuts to match, and the other country has nuts with no bolts to screw in. This is a situation with two stressful problems. Should the countries ignore their differences, and trade with each other, they will evolve into a situation where these two problems are simultaneously solved. This simple case illustrates the challenge of international trade. Unlike a unified nation, the community of countries is heterogeneous, representing incompatible cultures and varied moral values. So borders are maintained, and separate laws, customs, and regulations prevail. Every country will naturally insist on minting its own fiat currency because then it can manifest its control on its own destiny. It is for this reason that the theoretical musing about a universally accepted, international currency is still a lofty aspiration rather than an imminent reality. And that despite the many "bolts-nuts" situations in the international arena.

The advantage of a universal currency is overwhelming. One way to size it up is to imagine that each state in the United States would mint its own money, and the 50 currencies will trade daily, up and down. How much more complicated would life be in the United States? Project that on the 250 countries or so on this planet, trading each with its own currency. So we have, on one hand, the persistence of individual country currencies, and on the other hand, the attraction of a universal currency. What will be a good synthesis between these thesis and antithesis?

A cascade of digital currencies: We first digitize all the prevailing fiat currencies, namely, we digitize each currency into a binary string that reflects both value and identity. Second, we define derived digital currencies combined of pairs of digitized fiat currencies of two countries of strong mutual trade. For example, since the United States and Europe are heavy trade partners, we shall form a joint currency comprised of €1 and $1. This EuroDollar currency could be referenced in long-term bilateral trade agreements in order to alleviate the uncertainty of the relative values of euro versus dollar. Once the dollar and the euro are both digitized, it would be a simple matter to form that joint currency, and actually trade with it. Obviously, the joint EuroDollar currency would not harm neither the euro nor the dollar, and should enlist no objection neither from the US Federal Reserve nor from the European Central Bank. Bilateral agreements could be carried out with tethered money that reflects business arrangement, payment dates, payment conditions, etc. It would be the digitized EuroDollar that would be tethered. Similar bilateral "coins" will be minted for other bilateral trade. The next level will be to join such bilateral digital coins with another fiat currency or with another joint coin. This "higher up" or "cascaded" coin will find its use for projects that include contributors and participants from all the countries represented in this cascaded coin. As the use of these digital currencies spreads, so would the cascading process, and the respective tethering. Traders all over will have a choice of coin amalgams, and will gravitate toward a cascaded coin that would be based on the most trusted fiat currencies. Central banks will compete with each other to be considered trustworthy. In total, this digital currency cascading solution will serve as the synthesis solution to the above-mentioned dilemma: to allow smooth international trade while respecting the per country fiat currencies.

To implement such a cascade, it will be necessary to work with a public ledger of the exchange rates between the fiat currencies. With digital currencies, there is no arbitrage; we are all cyber neighbors. The dynamics of supply and demand will remain intact. Should someone mint a digital coin comprised of $3 and €1 (instead of the 1:1 before), and this coin will become popular, then traders will need to buy a lot of US dollars to purchase this coin. The price of the dollar will rise until the market will think that it's too high, and the value will stabilize. One may note that if a particular cascaded coin becomes really popular, it will become the norm, and used without the tedium of currency exchange.

Cascaded digital currencies will serve as most fitting money to accommodate business-to-business and peer-to-peer on an international scope. More and more projects involve contributors from many countries, and the Internet brings together individuals from far away, wishing to engage in a friendly exchange.

The Global Village cast together people and firms separated by lots of geography, and stretches of cultural differences, leading to mutual suspicion, and insistent apprehension. The fundamental way to account for these sentiments is to establish a cryptographic protocol fused to the digital money, such that no party can take advantage of the other. In other words, tethering is critical in promoting commercial and personal exchange across the globe. Cryptography recently developed a plethora of protocols designed to accommodate mutually mistrustful collaboration. A simple illustration for such a procedure is the case of Alice and Bob trying to share a pie. If Alice cuts the pie and gives Bob his share, then Bob might complain that his part is smaller than Alice's. But if the roles are reversed Alice may be the complainer. By using a procedure in which Alice cuts the pie, and Bob then selects the part he likes, then, as long as Alice and Bob remain rational, neither has any ground for disagreement; however, mistrustful they may be.

The cascaded currencies will be subject to normal market dynamics, and will be extendible beyond fiat currencies to precious metals, mineral reserves, real estate, etc. The cascade will climb up, creating joint currencies that would increasingly represent the wealth of humanity in total, and as such will be extremely stable, and even overwhelm other cascaded coins. In that case, such a super currency will be the choice tethered money especially for very long-term projects.

The intermint: Cascading is envisioned as a dynamic competitive market carried out through a web of mints (the intermint) that will adhere to a binding protocol to allow for a smooth interchange on a global scale.

International remittance: As this cascaded currencies phenomenon takes hold (depending on public acceptance, and on regulatory openness), tethered money may be applied to the imminent challenge of cheap and efficient international remittance. This is a half a trillion global market dominated by a few big players charging daunting fees for the service of shipping money from one country to the other. Digital money will fit the bill. Money will be texted, emailed, or otherwise electronically transported from the country of origin to the country of receipt. The recipient will have to redeem the digital money in a local digital money center that will be under the prevailing government supervision. All the regulations and restrictions will be encoded into the tethered remittance funds, and the local branch of the mint (perhaps a franchised bank) will not redeem the money until everything legally imposed on the transaction is being fulfilled.

* * *

Having run through some of the go-ready applications of tethered money, we now sit back and contemplate deeper meanings and possible long-range ramifications. Introducing the idea of financial democracy.

FINANCIAL DEMOCRACY (VOTING WITH OUR TAXES)

Twenty-five hundred years ago, a community called Athens introduced a simple idea that has emerged as the underlying basis for handling societal power in the modern world. The idea was that every member of a society has a contribution to make to what is going on in the society – has smarts to share, power to add, voice to be heard, responsibility to bear. A mechanism should be found to marshal the contributions of all, to account for the impact of everyone, to properly integrate the wishes and desires of the ordinary and extraordinary, of the commonplace and queer, of the agreeable and disagreeable. Chaotic as such regimen is, any alternative is worse. That is why we suffer the inefficiencies and the waste, the fraud, and the abuse rampant in the democratic process – because all alternatives are worse, as Winston Churchill pointed out.

This profound Greek idea has manifested itself through the "one-person-one-vote" election process and it has stayed this way for centuries now. Does it work? Does this mechanism fully express the profound idea of the ancient Athenians? We all know the story of antibiotics – it dealt a triumphant blow to killer bacteria, only that over the years the bacteria adapted and prevailed. New antibiotic is needed. Now what is the "bacteria" that the Athenians attacked? Their community-centric solution was a weapon against minority hold. They challenged any elite group – old, wise, rich, strong, well-birthed – and said, *you don't own us!* The monarchs, the despots, the emperors, and similar elite groups have been dealt a crashing blow, but like the killer bacteria they adapt, regroup, and they vie for power once more. Their main tool: money. Let us now introduce the specter for the community fighting back, deploying the new technology of tethered money.

Yes, we the people elect our leaders, so we have the power, don't we? Not really, not as much as we are taught we have. When we step into the voting booth to exercise our cherished power, we face a limited choice of candidates. How did this list of candidates come to be? It certainly does not include everyone who would like to present his or her candidacy. So who weeded out (or sanitized) the long list to the list we have to choose from? *Surely it's not us.* And surely the one who has the power to make the list from which we are to choose, has the power to give us the illusion of choosing, while retaining the same to itself. That invisible power is called money. One has to have, rent or buy financial muscle (selling promises, commitments, principles) to make it to that list. Our leaders then, while technically elected by us, society at large, are, *de facto*, the choice of those who have control of the money needed to reduce the original list of candidates to the voted-on list of candidates. These money brokers are the ones that decide our leaders by narrowing the voters' choices. And those leaders eventually levy taxes, and decide on their disposition. We have no choice not to comply with the tax code, and we have no say about the allocation of our taxes. It's only natural that those who enacted the laws to raise taxes, dispose of them in a self-serving manner. What else? Little wonder then that our taxes primarily serve the invisible financial power houses that get people elected, while sugarcoating us with the illusion that it is all for our benefit.

In reality, things are not so bleak, simply because good people do manage to crack the money chain, individuals of high character do get into office, and morality is not absent in the halls of power. But monarchies of old were not a monolith of evil and injustice either. There were enlightened despots, wise kings, and just rulers. We replaced them with democracy because the structure was flawed. And the structure of our modern day democracy is ill impacted by the invisible power of money.

Now here is a revolutionary idea that might be of some help in this quagmire. Instead of sending the Internal Revenue Service untethered money, we should send our taxes tethered to our preferred use of that money. Our tethering instructions don't have to be at a line-item resolution, they may be broad categories. Tethering may not apply to every dollar we surrender to the government; it may apply only to a fraction thereof. We should not go wild, but we may want to venture an experiment.

Suppose we decide that every taxpayer may tether 10% of his tax liability, to begin with. And suppose we further decree that for every tax dollar that is tethered an additional 15 cents of tax liability (tethered too) will be levied. This will amount to a taxpayer saying, I am ready to pay more taxes, if I have a say about their allocation. And suppose we allow taxpayers a limited tethering menu, say: "I disallow use of my tethered taxes to foreign aid", or "My tethered taxes will be fully allocated to medical research", or "I dedicate my tethered taxes to border security", etc. Such tethering will amount to practicing financial democracy. Financial democracy is a democracy-forte, where the populace not just casts a vote every 4 years, but also allocates resources throughout the 4 years. The technology is there, the actual implementation will need to experiment its way through a lot of trial and error for sure, but the principle is alluring:

a more faithful execution of the old Greek idea – society at large is where the power should reside.

It might even be that tax-tethering is the only way to stop politicians from mortgaging our future through unbridled borrowing. It might be the substitute for the lack of political will to cut back on entitlements. By initially limiting the tethering to a fraction of our tax liability, we insulate ourselves from any unexpected shock. Tethering money to a cause is a trustworthy technological solution. By comparison, voting for a politician that promised in a stump speech to favor our cause is extremely shaky, once the politician is in office, beholden to the powers that be.

Reality check: blue sky nice as this vote-with-your-taxes idea may be, it runs against serious obstacles. Budget allocation between competing options that require high level of expertise in order to distinguish between them, can hardly be trusted to crowd taste. By contrast, other choices reflect a moral compass, rather than expertise, and these choices are fit for vote with your taxes. A choice between a budget for nursing homes, as opposed to abortion clinics, is an example.

It might be easier to test run tethered taxes on a local level. The city of Rockville, Maryland, may prepare a list of "desired" (not "must have") projects, and the estimates for their completion, and then allow residents to tether say 5% of their taxes to a project of their choice. Only when the tethered taxes are enough, per the estimate of reference, is this project built. So if some "fat cats" would prefer a nice access road to the shopping mall they build, but the people will tether their money to a recreational park, then the people would prevail. Otherwise, the politicians who run on "fat cats" money will explain and argue that the access road is the best thing that can happen to the community.

The theme of financial democracy is not limited to tethered taxes. The public may vote with its money for any issue of concern. Tethering will strip the hidden power brokers from wielding their power, and the will of the people will prevail.

* * *

Tethered money technology allows for members of the public to tether small or large amounts of money to people and causes of their choice. This shifts the balance of hidden power – money power – to society at large. Much needed today when the act of political voting is no longer as effective as it used to be: big money found a way around it. It's time to fight back.

Chapter 3

Digital Money: The Security Nightmare

The early expressions of money, be it fancy seashells, bushels of barley or gold bars, had one attractive feature in common: it was practically impossible to fake them. You can steal gold, you can confiscate a ton of wheat, but you cannot fake seashells, barley or gold. You cannot make something else pass as money. Alas, when money was abstracted to banknotes, promissory notes, and other paper ware, it did gain tremendous efficiency, but it lost this sense of confidence against counterfeiting. And now, when *de facto* money becomes computerized data – the risk of making money out of thin air is almost as serious as stealing or robbing it from a place where it is there.

Today only 11% of the circulating money is reduced to coins and paper bills; the overwhelming majority of the funds are deposited in cyber space facing a strategic risk of a comprehensive catastrophe. How worrisome is that risk?

We all feel quite comfortable during our daily elevator ride. We trust that the cables that carry us will not snap. What is the basis of this trust? A testing lab has subjected similar cables to increasing forces until such time when the cables succumbed and tore apart. As long as the weight of a crowded elevator is way below that tearing force, the cable is expected to hold – that is science. By contrast, at best we have put a cyber financial system under a "white hats" attack, to see if we could commission some benevolent hackers to disrupt our money. If our security withstood the test, then we agree to sign off on our defensive measures and we "certify our money as secure." But that is like subjecting an elevator cable to the pull of a random rock, and if it holds, we assume that it would support the elevator. What if the elevator is heavier than the rock? The naked truth about cyber security is that it is a race of imagination. The security team performs threat analysis based on all the threat scenarios they can envision, and then they build answers to these threats – as best they can. But what if the assailants have more imagination? What if the hackers would conceive of an attack scenario that the defenders did not have the imagination to think of? And, as a result, they have failed to put up measures to defend from? There is one thing we clearly cannot control, but cannot discard, and that is the other side, the hackers, the attackers – our enemies, using an Alan Turing size mind on their behalf. Einsteins, Newtons, and Turings are not born exclusively in the West, and as we have seen in World War II, the singular contribution of one Alan Turing tipped the scales. Come to think about it, 9/11 was a failure of imagination: our enemies have conceived of an attack scenario that we did not have the imagination to foresee.

The truth of the matter is that the overwhelming advantage, efficiency and convenience of cyber finance leads us to accommodate this strategic risk. It prevails upon us to live with the nightmare of the financial calamity, as we do our best to meet the challenge.

Alas, a pervasive school of thoughts calls for hiding this risk reality, papering it over with reassuring statements, suppressing its scope. The argument is that the public will fail to realize the subtleties of the situation, and freeze its cyber financial activities. Even worse: some fear a movement of retreating to gold and other noncybersized currencies, sending waves of havoc over the entire civil order.

Such "panic effect" arguments are not without merit, but the suppression of the scope of the risk cast any attempt to address the fundamental risk, as excessive and unduly alarmist. Especially with regard to expensive security measures. The suppressers also point out that a major catastrophe has never occurred. It is like the argument that, I never got a heart attack before, why should I worry about it now.

Our financial leaders are by and large economists not computer scientists, so they focus their attention on interest rates, liquidity, currency wars, etc. What is needed is to properly assess the combined threat on our financial order, and accurately appraise its cyber component. The more accurately and measurably we assess the cyber risk, the better our chances to meet its challenge.

This chapter will discuss financial cyber threat, and make the case that reforming money as a digital string is a move that would harness, fence-in, and alleviate the risk to our financial well being – contrary to some knee-jerk opinions.

CYBER INSECURITY: ALWAYS WITH US!

The twentieth century began with a tantalizing spirit of triumph of the mind, the ascendance of order, rationality, and explicability. Physics was an (almost) done science, math was on the verge of proving its perfection, the bottom of knowledge appeared within reach. Soon enough though, Albert Einstein has shown that Newton described but the corridor of science, Gödel proved that confusion and inconsistency are irrepressible in math, Niels Bohr concluded that nature is a casino driven by probabilities, and Alan Turing demonstrated that we cannot foretell what a computer program will do. All in all, nature and computing is a rich hiding place for surprises, sudden turns, and unsettling mysteries; a hiding place so readily shared by a malevolent agent.

Let us focus on Alan Turing. In 1936, he wrote a paper that was largely ignored at the time (Turing, 1936). In his paper Turing described a remarkably simple apparatus, which came to be called a Turing machine. A full description of the machine is contained in just three paragraphs ahead. Yet, this simple machine was proven by Turing to be able to compute anything computable. This powerful proof means that any conclusion regarding computing (and computing security) drawn from a Turing machine would stand valid with respect to our servers, work stations, desktops, laptops, tablets, and smartphones. The Turing machine as described by Turing was never practically built, but it guided and inspired all the various computers that changed our lives since the mid-1940s.

The universality of Turing machine suggests another interesting conclusion: anyone comprehending the subsequent paragraphs – understands how computers work, and will readily understand why computers suffer from persistent cyber insecurity challenges.

The Alan Turing machine is a box that accepts a single natural number as input, and produces a single natural number as output. Each of these two numbers is expressed as a series of symbols (e.g., 5-9-3-1-1-9-7) written on a tape. The input tape is fed to the box where a read/write head is reading the symbol now under it, then the head may rewrite another symbol at that spot, followed by either moving the tape one symbol to the right, or moving it one symbol to the left, or leaving the tape where it is.

This read/write head may also rotate perpendicular to its writing direction and move from one rotating position to another. What the read/write head does when a symbol is placed under it, is determined by its rotating position. After re-writing a symbol, and yanking the tape in one direction of the other (or none), the read/write tape may change its rotational position.

Inside the read/write head there exist rules that say what is to be done when the rotational position is r, and the symbol below is s. If what's to be done is to halt the process then the Turing machine stops, and the tape contains the computational output corresponding to the input as it was written on the tape originally. If it does not stop, then it failed, so far, to compute the answer, and in general, one cannot tell whether the machine will eventually halt or not.

That's it – the Turing machine is fully described. With enough "rules" of the same format, in the read/write head, and with a tape as long as necessary, the Turing machine can do what any other computer can. Turing's genius can be appreciated as the mind that described the above "machine" and then had the insight to realize that for no conceivable computational task will there be a need to use a more complicated arrangement.

A Turing machine is essentially sequential; the sequence of steps is decided together by the set of "commands" in the box and the data marked on the tape. Neither the commands alone, nor the tape alone will determine the next steps. Turing was able to prove that for anything computable there is a combination of a finite tape, a finite set of commands, operating on a finite size alphabet that together, step by step, computes an answer to any given input. The watchword here is "finite." The fundamental distinction between computer science and math is found right here in this word. Mathematicians speak casually on infinity, even on "grades of infinity," while with computers everything is finite. And because of that it would appear that one could foretell if a Turing machine will halt at some point, or continue its steps in perpetuity. Turing dashed this intuition, proving, way back in 1936 that one has to run the program, carry out the steps, in order to prove that it halts, or stay puzzled about it as long as it does not. The implications for computer security are that one has to run (or simulate the running) of a computer to find a well-hidden subtle malware – there is no mathematical shortcut!

THE GENERAL PURPOSE COMPUTER AND ITS INHERENT INSECURITY

Von Neumann and his fellow mathematicians at The Princeton Institute for Advanced Studies, became quite annoyed at the inconvenience of waiting for electrical engineers to build up the hardware on which to run their computation, and so they steered the budding computing enterprise toward the idea of building generic hardware and save the specifics of every program to the software. This would alleviate the dependency of the mathematicians on the engineers. We see this trend triumphant today: our laptop, our tablets, our phones are pieces of hardware on which a vast variety of software is operating – including the software written by our unfriendly hackers. To the extent that greater portions of the program logic would be carried out in hardware (special purpose computers), that is the extent to which cyber security will improve.

The hardware that supports virtually all our computers is totally in the open, and pretty exposed to all programmers – to the "white hats" and the "black hats." This standardization is very convenient for us, but in the same token – very dangerous too. Our order, streamlined operation, and predictability is the stuff the hackers abuse. To the extent that we use variety and inject unpredictability, that is the extent to which hackers would be restricted and curtailed.

A hacker, say, in Latvia, aiming for J.P. Morgan, would be equipped with the *a priori* knowledge of which servers the bank uses, which database products, which firewalls, which operating systems, and which communication gear. He would know what the J.P. Morgan computers would do in reaction to any data, or software he manages to send in. Computer viruses propagate so efficiently because the virus knows exactly how it would be processed, everywhere it hits. So on one hand the general-purpose computer allows us to write software and generate a variety of capabilities, but on the other hand it is this very universality of the machine that empowers the assailants of our data assets. We marvel how our smartphone can talk, text, do email, tell the news, the weather, the stock market, read our books aloud, book our next flight, pay our bills – hardly realizing that this universal platform is what the data thieves so conveniently exploit!

The problem of standardization is especially acute with respect to finance. To effect smooth global money transfer, the platform must be standardized, and be very predictable. This issue is a bit easier with respect to digital money, since it can be stored and accounted for internally in a private way; only the transfer of money must be negotiated and agreed across the network.

COMPLEXITY: WHERE SECURITY AND INSECURITY MEET

If there is one term that is the key to understand the security issues of modern computerized finance, it is the term *complexity*: how we manage it, how we use it to shield our money data, and how it hides our most lethal cyber threats.

Our civil order is based on our intensive free exchange of value – a smooth dynamics of payments and trade. If we are prevented from buying and selling what we need, and what we produce, then we can't function, and we can't maintain the civil order in the country.

Albeit, as of now, payment gets easier, banking smoother, money flows faster, and nearly every personal electronic gadget has turned into a click-ready payment gate. We build new, ever more complicated, financial instruments; we spread risk wisely; and we regard the whole world as a local market. We also integrate in leaps and bounds: no more regional boundaries, even national boundaries become blurry – cross border, cross currency, cross dependence. We do everything that large complex systems do, before they explode or implode, or deflate, or spiral down – whatever forms the rapid loss of stability takes. We are blind to the warning signs. We play wild in the Titanic casino, mindless of the coming encounter with the deadly iceberg. The out of bound complexity frightens too many of our economic leaders who resort to the old tricks with a paralysis of thought and with a dearth of innovation. Typically, governments on an economic slide resort to printing more money because it solves the problem of the hour. It's like the crowd climbing up the rising stern of the Titanic, gets you further from the water.

So what are we to do?

We should use the calm before the storm to do what the storm will prevent us from doing: *deliberate*. We should ask fundamental questions, propose strategic changes, and explore risk-reduction options. I submit that digital currency, and in particular tethered digital currency, deserves a very serious consideration as a fundamental alternative to the risky cyberframe we operate today. Digital currency will eliminate the vast majority of system penetration risks we encounter in our present system; it will redraw the monetary security battleground around the mints, and limit it there. A similar advantage will be extracted from the cryptographic front. Today, our electronic money relies on mathematically unproven, constantly weakening ciphers. Digital money can be issued without this vulnerability. Another advantage afforded by digital currency is based on the option to cover the field with several mints (The Intermint), allowing for quick disengagement from a fatally injured particular mint. These points will be elaborated on, in this chapter. The security advantages inherent in the digital money paradigm amounts to an independent, strong argument in its favor, even without the use and impact of tethered digital money discussed in Chapter 2.

COMPLEXITY: HOW DO WE MANAGE IT TODAY?

This book has been written with the claim that money has enabled the most powerful human phenomenon: division of labor, which in turn allowed different people to migrate to their natural best, and tinkerers and thinkers were able to exercise their talent and move civilization forward. Hand in hand with this division of labor, humanity exercised an equally important development: *division of knowledge.* Early on, when we all were farmers, we shared pretty much the same knowledge (also earlier, when we all joined in a hunt). But once some of us worked in the foundry and fashioned iron tools, the body of human knowledge expanded, but it was no longer shared. The blacksmith did not keep up with farming knowledge, and the farmer was quite ignorant about how to fashion a plough shed.

Today our division of knowledge is highly advanced. We enjoy the benefits and comfort of modern living without more than a shallow understanding as to how it all comes about. We drive our cars ignorant about the systems under the hood, we operate a computer with only abstract knowledge of what is going on inside. We fly to our destination despite ignorance about the mechanics of flying, or the complexity of managing an airport. Alas, if we all had to be fully aware of the details of all our actions, we would have not gone very far, nor been able to handle any meaningful complexity.

Indeed our ingenious way for handling complexity is to wrap a piece of operational knowledge in a proverbial box, about which we learn what input we have to feed it, and where to fetch the output from. By doing so, we need only high level functional knowledge of what happens in the box, enough to know what input is expected, and what to do with its output, but nothing further.

IBM was leading the computer industry in 1960s, with a concept called HIPO that meant hierarchical input process output. It expressed the amazing, successful, and durable IBM design philosophy: a computer system has a well-defined input, well-defined output, and a process that leads from one to the other. The process was depicted as a box, often called *black box*, to indicate the fact that the party that feeds the input to the box and then reads the output, does not have to know how the box cooks the former to the latter. The letter "H" hierarchical in HIPO was critical too; it said that if one cracks the box open what she sees is a few or more smaller black boxes inter-wired such that the output of one box serves as input to another. And the wires eventually show how the input to the just cracked box leads to its output. And when any one of these small boxes is cracked open, the view is essentially the same inter-wired still smaller boxes. This hierarchical configuration may continue to any desired depth until at some point the last boxes don't have smaller boxes under them. This HIPO principle is how we manage complexity – computerized or otherwise.

Why is it so ingenious? Because not only do sister boxes practice mutual ignorance, the parent box may be completely ignorant about the doings of their children boxes. So, while a musical symphony is composed by a composer who knows every note and every bar in it, and it is conducted by a conductor with equal knowledge of every note, the "symphony," called the Internet has no single maven that controls or is aware of all its operational details. HIPO allows us to manage complexity using a bunch of rather simple-minded people who know each one box in the complexity. We use the division of knowledge that money led us to, and practice *recombinant knowledge* to achieve unlimited technological feats. That is how we landed a man on the moon. I worked at NASA, sitting in on design sessions where a dozen of experts with mutual ignorance put together a winning design.

But what happens when just one among all those who come together to build complexity harbors an adversarial aim?

The mutual ignorance configuration allows a single adversary masquerading as a friend, to afflict untold damage. Let's consider one tiny "box, as described above." All that it does is multiply. When activated, the box opens two "mail boxes," or let's call them "input trays" one marked X, the other marked Y. The box then multiplies the numeric contents of these boxes and deposits the result in its output tray, marked Z. This multiplication box serves a higher (in the hierarchy) box that often deposits a numeric value into X and Y, then activates the multiplier box, and fetches the result $Z = X \times Y$ from the Z output tray.

Let's further say that the multiplier box is a slice of an integrated circuit that was ordered from a far away country. Because of that, we decide to check it out thoroughly. We use a random number generator and deposit random pairs into trays X and Y. We then compute the value of Z independently from the multiplier box, and compare the box's output with our own calculation. We are thorough, so we test this little box 1,000,000 times! Every time the result is exactly what we expect. This successful test plan arms us with sufficient confidence to install this chip in a most crucial financial system where multiplication is very often needed.

Alas, suppose that the manufacturer of this multiplier chip is a sworn enemy of this country, so he builds the chip to provide the right answer except that in one case the chip will do some harm. This case is when X = 11,740,992,234 and

Y = 51,253,919,597. Given that one could deposit in trays X and Y any number, say between 0 and 2^{53} (JavaScript norm) it figures out that in one million tests the chance of catching this malware is one to a billion times billion – negligible. In other words, even such a tiny operational box (multiplication) may be contaminated with malware that has a very strong chance to remain undetected. And given the fact that a simple computing environment has millions of mutually ignorant functional boxes, it is easy to see that malware has many hiding places, and with a bit of evil imagination a host of nasty surprises may afflict us.

One may notice that the way this array of functional boxes works is that each box refers to an input tray from where to fetch its input. Now, much as the agent which deposits the input and reads the output (not necessarily the same agent) knows only the functional relationship between the output and the input (at best) but is unaware of the operational details of how the former transforms into the latter, so it is for the processing box itself, in reference to the contents of its input tray. The box is clueless as to who deposited contents into its input trays. If an evil-minded agent manages to sneak in and secure control of the computing machine, then it can replace the bona fide contents of the input tray with a different value, and the processing box will not be the wiser.

Money, in modern computing systems, is a number written in an input tray, or more generically, a number written into a computer address. Anyone with proper access may change the value of the amount of money. It may be my account, or it may be yours.

But why can't we stop the bad guys from accessing our computer?

There are two fundamental answers to this question: (1) remote access and identity management and (2) the data/software shared storage.

REMOTE ACCESS AND IDENTITY MANAGEMENT

In order to operate the fantastic payment *anywhere-anytime* regimen we enjoy today, we have no choice but to allow individuals, machines, and software to gain access and control of far away computing machines. With billions of instances daily, of access from around the world to hundreds of thousands of financial computers, the chances for a mishap is too high to ignore. And yes, we do have security measures, and some are quite sophisticated. We have many solutions to the challenge of identity verification, which nonetheless remains one of the pesky lingering challenges of distributed computing today. How can Alice verify that her communication partner, who claims to be Bob, is indeed Bob, and not Mr Hack from Evilville? If Alice and her remote partner would have been sitting face-to-face, then Alice would have had a practically unlimited stream of information projecting from her communication partner – his looks, his behavior, his reactions, his voice, even his smell. She would also have had her built-in brainy "software," developed over millions of years of evolution, designed to identify her friends. But positioned remotely from her communication partner, all that she has before her is a limited stream of bits. If that stream contains the expected bits, Alice's software will conclude that she talks with Bob. If Mr Hack from Evilville somehow manages to deduce, or to guess, the right sequence of bits then he will be regarded as Bob for all concerns and purposes. With hundreds of millions of identity verification instances daily, a nonnegligible portion thereto is fraudulent. The means to verify an identity are cryptographic in nature; cryptography offers a distinction between key holders and nonkey holders, where a key is any piece of secret information. The key can be lost, stolen, and guessed in ways too numerous to account for. Hackers install keyloggers on target computers: software that copies the full sequence of keyboard activity, and then sends it to a hacker. A very diligent and careful high government official was accused of not guarding his high security access password. He denied the accusation. It was eventually found out that one late night the same official logged on to a private membership account, and tired as he was, he keyed in his government access code. The membership account rejected it; the official quickly recognized his mistake and corrected it. Only that a hacker installed software that captured all failing passwords, having had the imagination to expect that exact scenario. How can this be prevented – by not logging on while tired? A wily hacker dined in a fancy restaurant, and checked out immediately after a "loaded looking lady" did. An hour later, he called the restaurant pretending to be Visa security, gave the particulars of his own transaction, and thereby established his "Visa security" credentials, asking and receiving the particulars of the previous check out. It's the imagination race, and the identity thieves may fail a thousand times before succeeding once, but once is enough to start the climb to even higher credentials, with even more destructive power in the maze of hundreds of thousands of financial institutions.

Once the hackers are in, we have quite a good chance to catch them over time, as they roam around and sow harm. We have sophisticated pattern recognition tools that identify a hacker-like behavior, as opposed to a bona fide user's behavior. But even if we flush out a hacker, it is quite difficult to play back his moves from the point of penetration, and undo all the damage that he afflicted. What is more, some smart hackers get in to a central system and then stay put; and only very infrequently come out, exercise their evil doing, maybe very subtly, before silently return to hiding. In some ways, the small blows are more devastating than the big ones. Because of the great concern for the integrity of the monetary system in this country, it is mandatory for all financial institutions to be very diligent with layers of back-ups that can be called back if the front data is corrupt. And indeed, if a virus wipes out an entire disk, the back-up is invoked. But what if the malware withdraws money from slumbering accounts where the owner is not paying too much attention, and only much later, if ever, a complaint is raised? And then countless work hours must be devoted to disentangle the theft trajectory. Or what if the hacker introduces small fake transactions into many credit card statements. Most people will overlook these charges, and those who spot them are likely to be too lazy to dispute them (the banks make it as difficult as reasonably possible to dispute a charge).[1]

Recently, and with great fanfare, a new technology appeared to have dealt a fatal blow to the people from Evilville – *biometric identification*. The technology is impressive and powerful, and is very effective for people in a face-to-face situation, proving their identity, like the palm readers, in passport stations. But it has no real added value, rather the opposite, for remote identification. First, it only works to identify people, not organizations. Second, whatever the biometric, its data is eventually encapsulated in a digital string (a biometric signature), which is compared to the signature in the verifying database. Once a hacker steals this data extract of a fingerprint, he no longer needs to chop off his victim's thumb to steal his identity, as shown in some horror movies. And because people are so falsely confident with this biometric, and thus less careful with other measures, the net result may be negative.

The identity verification dilemma may bite us hard when it applies to major transactions. Normally, a bank will not accept an incoming wire from another bank without a very elaborate identity verification protocol. However elaborate, the protocol calls for a limited sequence of bits. When a hacker emulates the expected sequence, he can send himself, or to a cohort, an impressive fake wire, take the money, and disappear.

The risk picture is even more serious when the communicating parties are abstract constructs, rather than breathing, sweating human beings. When corporations transact with other constructs, like LLC, hedge funds, or any other sophisticated financial entity, the identification challenge is greater because unlike human beings which are, by their nature, an indefatigable source of identification data, abstract constructs are totally defined by a finite, usually quite small, number of well ordered bits. While an n bits string is likely to be guessed right with only a small chance of 2^{-n}, the reality is that identification strings are of low entropy, they have a well-known built-in order, and the chance to figure out their id is much larger. Once a hacker, so succeeds, the potential damage may be grandiose.

To summarize, our computing environment is fundamentally limited to handling a finite number of bits, which is all that we have at our disposal, to apply to the challenge of identifying our remote communication partner. This limitation creates an irreducible lingering risk. The risk is even greater when the communicating partners are abstract entities themselves, and when software transactions are exercised hundreds of millions of times a day. Money flow today is based on identifying both the payer and the payee. If one or both parties are misidentified, the money flows to or from the wrong account.

---

1. My son, Yaron, started a company, BillGuard, focused on spotting unwanted credit card charges. As a proud father, I had to mention it here.

Big Data, Not Always so Big

"Big Data Analytics" is one of the "coolest" tech-terms in 2015, referring to algorithms that slice and dice reams of data, to elicit conclusions and relationships not known, not even suspected before. Such "data mining" systems are routinely applied to the mountains of financial data: to catch theft and fraud. The idea being that since so much data accumulates daily, there is more and more "beef" to process, in order to characterize an identity thief, for example. This is indeed so, insightful relationships may be discovered by combing reams of relevant data. Alas, too often the technology is over-applied leading to useless conclusions and unhelpful relationships that while they are covered by a validity fig-leaf, their inference is misleading. This is for the same reason that pure random data would yield "big data" conclusions, and "analytic" relationships, which in fact reflect normal randomized variety. You will hardly hear this admitted by Big Data vendors and proponents, who claim that "big data tools" offer the magic of deriving conclusions over a subject without ever understanding what it is about. It is a triumph of raw data over modeling and case insight: which is both its strength and weakness.

THE DATA/SOFTWARE SHARED STORAGE

In the early days of computing a debate raged between those who wished to allocate separate storage for data and separate storage for active programs on one hand, and those who wanted to mix them, on the other hand. The latter prevailed and in today's architecture the same storage space where we house our data, we also house our active software. This solution has proven itself very useful in many ways but, at the same time, it was thoroughly exploited by the hackers' community. As a matter of fact, the underlying idea behind the plague called computer virus is that a malicious virus is comprised of code that afflicts harm, and then it copies itself as pure data to be stored until it is invoked and it afflicts the harm again, on the same or different computer.

The 89% of money today is never reduced to anything more tangible than a figure placed in a computer address. The computer address is associated with an account. An account is a union between an owner and a sum of money. So, an owner (individual or a business entity) "points" to an address, and the address is a computer location where a number is written, and that number represents a dollar amount that is credited to the owner who points to that address. Virtually, all the money that circulates in our economy is so represented. And this representation occurs in servers that are routinely and extensively exposed to a community of access hounds from all over the world, from all corners of the Internet. We have seen that identity verification is a daunting challenge, and once hackers are in, they cause harm in myriads of ways. They can change the identity of the owner who points to an address as his or hers. They can change the number in the address that carries the money, before or after the black box operated on it. Hackers have smartly exploited the mutual ignorance methodology in handling complexity (HIPO) and introduced into any number of deep-seated black boxes some hidden malware that lays dormant until they are awakened. Who knows how many of these dormant "hobbits" lurk in the HIPO-structured bulk of our worldwide financial software?

The integrity of the financial system is maintained via countless applications of the simple rules of conservation – for any account that shows an increment of some x dollars, there must be one or more accounts where the total decrement of dollars sums up to x. It's getting quite complicated because the incrementing and decrementing accounts may be on far off, poorly communicating systems. Sometimes the delay in money accounting is detrimental in flashing out inconsistency and, in many instances, it is very complicated to find out the root cause for books imbalance. Hackers may keep the conservation laws intact, but afflict untold damage by establishing faked transactions between accounts. A bigger fear is that hackers will be smart enough to "print money": overcome the meticulous and secret means designed to prevent hackers from generating money from thin air, and ruin the system.

In its essence, it is the mutual ignorance methodology that we use to handle complexity that is also the grounds for our dread that the easy abstract money we so enjoy handling today will come to a catastrophic halt.

Slowly and persistently, more and more financial security experts express concern regarding the inherent vulnerability of our financial base. The White House and other Federal agencies came to admit that much of what we do is ad hoc. The hackers compromise our system, and we react with a patch. They move to the next trick, and we respond with a second patch. That is not a fountain of comfort. A call has been issued for academic institutes to come up with a comprehensive theory for financial security. This is a tacit way of admitting that we are really worried that all this smooth comfort of global financial flow is not as robust as most of us believe that it is.

COMPLEXITY USED AS A SHIELD

In the previous section we described money as a number written in a "storage spot" – an address. We protect the integrity of our money – this number – by protecting the box, the address where it resides. We have an impressive array of locks and walls and fences designed to shield our stored money, our stored data, from thieves. Albeit, money has to move in order to fulfill its mission. It has to leave the safety of its protective box and be exposed in transit. As we have seen, what we do today, is not moving money *per se* but moving software instructions that have the effect of incrementing the money number in the payee box, and decrementing it in the payer's box. But nonetheless these software instructions, as they rush from one payment party to another, are out of the box and fully exposed.

In the early days, the thought was to extend the physical and functional protection to the channels where the payment data was flowing. Large corporations and banks built their private physical networks for the purpose. This strategy was soon abandoned when it became clear that no private network could compete with the speed, robustness, versatility, outreach, and cost efficiency of the Internet. But the Internet is the *public* information highway. Once our money data is released to travel across the Internet, we do not know what path it would take, what hubs it would visit, who will see it, and who will modify or kill it. Our money data is exposed, no more box protection. Instead we have devised a more intimate protection: *encryption.* Encryption protects data not by surrounding it with a shield, but by injecting complexity into it, so that unintended readers will be lost in this complexity, and not be able to read the plaintext the way it was before complexity was applied to it.

The advantage of the cryptodefense is that it is applied to the data (the money if you will) itself, not to its storage place. If a storage box is compromised, the content of the box is exposed. But, if data is processed with complexity induction, then it is shielded by this complexity wherever it goes, Internet or otherwise.

The simplest and oldest means of complexity injection is transposition: mixing the letters into a different order. The word TABLE, for instance, will be sent out as BELAT. Since the word "TABLE" has 5 letters, we have $5! = 5 \times 4 \times 3 \times 2 = 120$ permutations, and it won't be too difficult to unravel. However, consider the phrase "MOM SET UP THE TABLE" which is comprised of 20 letters. Now the number of permutations climbs to: $20! = 20 \times 19 \times 18 \times \cdots \times 2 = 2.4329 \times 10^{18}$ which makes it quite more complex to unravel the ciphertext: "ETB LT MESAP OUT HME" to its corresponding plaintext. Clearly though, the complexity shield works even under the assumption of complete exposure of the ciphertext.

The entire field of mainstay cryptography, through all its ciphers, algorithms, schemes, and tricks, may be described as means to impose complexity and intractability on our adversaries.

It is noteworthy that the basic framework of cryptography, as it was framed in antiquity, has survived the fast march of technology without much of a change. Cryptography deals with something called an "alphabet," which may be the literal English alphabet, or a much longer list, as in modern ciphers, based on large numbers modular arithmetic. A plaintext is simply some sequence of letters from the chosen alphabet. To inject complexity, we invent a mechanism to change the letters in the plaintext with other letters of the same or a different alphabet (not necessarily one letter with one letter, and not necessarily the same exchange in every occurrence of the plaintext letter). When all the letters are exchanged, we have constructed a sequence of the exchanged letters, which we call the output of the cryptographic complexity injection; in most (but not all) cases, the product is called the ciphertext.

The intended reader of our plaintext has a piece of information called "key" with which he or she can remove the complexity, restore the plaintext, and interpret our message. We assume that everyone else, especially our adversary, does not have possession of the key – did not steal it, nor extract it unwittingly from the intended reader. We regrettably acknowledge that with sufficient persistence and efforts, the complexity we have so deliberately injected into the message can be removed (exposing the original plaintext). Yet we still hope, believe, and trust that the effort needed to do so, (to remove the complexity), is too hard, takes too long, and costs too much money, and therefore our adversary will hopefully not even try to read our message. And, if he tries he will run out of money before he succeeds, or conclude that it would cost him too much compared to the expected value of extracting the plaintext, or if he keeps trying and spending money on it, then it would take him so long that by the time he removes the injected complexity, it will do him no good and do us no harm. This assumption is underlying all our cryptographic measures, regardless of which cipher we use, which algorithm we apply, or which protocol is selected – this assumption is universal to the entire field of crypto complexity.

Having established that for data in transit, the complexity shield is our sole defense, we must ask ourselves how trustworthy is the assumption that the complexity is complex enough.

Examining the validity of this assumption is critical because all our data assets, including money (money is data these days), rely on this basic assumption. Our examination leads to the conclusion that this assumption is solid and trustworthy if, and only if (1) our adversaries are not smarter than we are and (2) they will not innovate a solution within the time in which they can still cause us harm.

This conclusion is critical and in good conscience, we must insure a precise elucidation of its implications.

Complexity, like beauty, is in the eyes of the beholder. Many psychologists though, tried to canonize beauty and map it on a scale – not much success there. Similarly, mathematicians feverishly tried, for decades now, to develop an objective measure for complexity. It was a desire to quantify complexity regardless of the smarts of its attacker. Some claim that this long arduous effort was doomed to fail, to begin with. Described provocatively (but accurately), this effort amounts to saying: *what we – smart that we are – think is difficult, intractable, and complex – is also difficult, intractable, and complex for anyone, however smarter, however more insightful.* We fail to notice that on a very profound level, the meaning of wisdom and insight is to discern a solution, a way out, where less insight and poorer wisdom concludes despair.

If you ask a locksmith if he has a single method that would guarantee to crack every lock, the locksmith would likely shrug and say "Not exactly ..." But if you place in front of him a particular lock (not "lock" in abstraction) then, if he is good, he would tinker and tinker, until he cracks it. A similar subtle situation we have with mathematical complexity. Even if our adversary will not be in possession of a general algorithm that would fastcrack any number to its two prime factors, for some particular such number, used in a particular implementation of, say, RSA, there may be a "private" solution for a large subset of the cases, and which is based on some hidden attributes that we are not aware of, but our adversary has already discovered. *It is even unwise to determine with declared confidence the boundaries of he who is wiser; and he who does so, does not understand the nature of wisdom.*

Because cryptography is so heavily mathematical, most people think that when the US government declares, say, AES or RSA as "secure ciphers," it follows that government mathematicians have come up with a proof to back-up their recommendation. A mathematical proof is the best that we can come up with, in terms of imposing restrictions on people smarter than we are.[2] But the bare truth is that we have no such proof whatsoever. We do have a solid proof that all the recommended ciphers are breakable, and hence the secret they protect is discoverable to our adversaries. As to how fast they will be in compromising our secrets – for that we have only our own subjective experience as guide. For a cipher to be recommended for use, it must be submitted to aggressive attacks by as many cryptographers as possible, and if they fail, they declare the cipher as robust. This state of affairs qualifies for the disturbing statement that we rely on our arrogance to declare a cipher as "recommended for use." Essentially what the recommendation committee is saying is: "Since we tried and could not crack this cipher, and since we are the smartest mathematicians around, then it follows that our adversaries, who are clearly dumber than we are, will surely find this cipher too complex to handle."

What is more, this spirit of arrogance, repeated itself throughout the history of cryptography. Developers of new complex ciphers are, as a matter of course, overconfident that their newfound complexity will baffle their adversaries, only to find out that history repeats itself and their complexity is not so complex after all. The most glaring example is the German Enigma cipher, which fortunately for the Allies, was used with a sense of overconfidence throughout World War II, while a British team in Bletchley Park, near London, headed by Alan Turing had routinely cracked the German messages and prospectively shortened the war by about 2 years.

Complexity is a very tricky and beguiling notion. In one way, it is strongly related to intelligence. Some notions of math and physics that I would find exceedingly complex would appear laughingly simple to Albert Einstein. If you ask me what day of the week corresponds to, say, November 15, 2086, I would scratch my head, but it is quite well known that for certain people this is a trivial question. Similarly, if you ask me to factor the number 2,160,807,217 to its two multipliers: $2,160,807,217 = 45,841 \times 47,137$, I would have to sweat on it

---

2. Some argue that even a mathematical proof is subjective, but the framework of this writing will not allow us to digress there. Come to think about it, all proofs of math and all statements of science were issued by a human brain, which as we now know, is a product of Darwinian evolution, and by its nature is happenstance, driven by survival, not by objective knowledge of reality. So how skewed are we, how deviant from the abstract notion of objective knowledge? See my book "Unbound Ignorance."

for a while. But, I would stop short of claiming that no one in the universe can solve this problem much faster. And yet, this particular math problem is exactly the complexity that underlies the most popular asymmetric cipher: RSA (albeit with much larger numbers).

Let us put intelligence aside for a moment. Let's suppose that our adversaries are not smarter than we are, and since we found it difficult to resolve a given complexity, so would they. *Fine, but what about innovation?*

Innovation is a process that provides us tomorrow with solutions we do not possess today. Innovation is the belief that insight can be developed, understanding can emerge, and complexity can dissolve – it is just a matter of effort. The RSA complexity mentioned earlier – factoring a large number – is one, which is constantly eroding. Every few months, a new article is published with a faster method to achieve the stated goal. Who can predict the residual complexity of RSA (and of any other cipher, for that matter) over any reasonable future? Just think of the irony: we regard ourselves as living in the age of innovation, and here, regarding the very foundation of our innovation fueled life – electronic finance – we base our confidence and functional well-being on a bold bet *against* innovation. We bet that in the foreseeable future, our adversaries will not be able to innovate a shortcut around the complexity that we challenge them with.

The RSA company put up a monetary prize (it started as a $10,000 prize, now it's much higher) for anyone who can factor a number fast enough. And lo and behold, nobody stepped up to collect. Isn't it a *de facto* proof that innovation is bunk, that there are no super brilliant people around? Let's recall the story of the German Enigma. Winston Churchill was so anxious to suppress any suspicion on the part of the Nazis that their prized cipher was compromised, that he reportedly, sacrificed the city of Coventry in November 1940. He ordered the Royal Air Force off the city, allowing the Luftwaffe to destroy its historical buildings and kill over 500 people. Had the Germans suspected the truth they would have added complexity to the Enigma, or replaced it altogether. The same reality rules today. Having spent what must be an enormous amount of effort to crack, say RSA, an adversary would not brag about it and claim the prize, but rather exploit the feat, compromise our data, all in sufficiently restricted measures to suppress any suspicion on our side.

What is more? Only a tiny fraction of the world community of professional cryptographers operates in the public eye and publishes its work. The overwhelming majority operates behind heavy curtains of secrecy. What they do, how much they know, what cipher they have cracked – *is everybody's guess.*

The United States is the sole remaining superpower in the world – a state of affairs that ticks off just about everybody else. Countries around the world that foresee themselves on a prospective collision course with the United States would readily realize that most of them have little chance to match the US Army, US Navy, or US Air force; but, on the other hand, the United States is the most vulnerable country in cyberspace, so it is only natural for those countries to focus on their cyber weapons. How many countries have already contaminated our civil and military database systems, keeping dormant agents in our servers and networks – ready for the day hostilities break? These countries will surely search for their Einstein or Turing, and keep them working in complete secrecy. And, we are not the wiser. Lured into dangerous relaxation of our alertness and seduced by the convenience of today's payment dynamics, we may be sitting ducks, naked and vulnerable.

Nobody knows for sure whether our mainstay ciphers have all been compromised, or are about to. There will be no telltale signs. What we know from recent natural disasters is that our electronic payment heaven can overnight become payment hell. Our money assets are mostly data entries in computer storage locations. Our payment ease is based on 24/7 ready access to our accounts and on instantly executable payment orders to sell or buy. Once payments stop because the crypto complexity defense has been melted away, or the server that holds our money has been brought down by trusted computer orders that were concocted by our adversaries who used our compromised ciphers – then our civil order, as we know it, will undergo a major disruption.

So why don't we hear about it, you wonder? Well, those who listen well, do hear some very disturbing proclamations voiced by the President, the Secretary of Defense, the NSA chief, etc. The risk of an "IT Pearl Harbor," or of a "Cyber 9/11" is mentioned quite often. What is not highly advertised are the bare facts presented herein that we rely on no mathematical proof when we use crypto complexity to process our data; but on hope, trust, and arrogance. If that were to be advertised, then the public might not bank online, and the banks would have to build more and more branches and hire more and more tellers. E-commerce would be more timid and the efficiency of cloud computing would be overshadowed by the vulnerability of cryptography.

Having sounded the alarm over the state of present day cipher systems, it is important to note that while these ciphers should be regarded with caution and suspicion, they should not be dismissed. For one reason – that they enable the amazing global experience and work efficiency we witness today. Much as we don't return to horse and buggy, despite the over 10,000,000 US motor vehicle accidents every year, with over 30,000 fatalities, so we should not retreat from our state of cyber progress because the ciphers we use are vulnerable. We should account for their vulnerability and there are very effective means to do so, once we realize it is necessary.[3]

The most innovative idea that emerged in cryptography in the past decades is the surprise solution to cryptography between strangers. For centuries, cryptography was practiced by two parties who knew each other beforehand and had a chance to exchange a shared key. Then came the Internet and transformed the planet into a fully interconnected village, allowing strangers to find each other

---

3. See my book "The Unending CyberWar."

and do business. Alas, to execute an electronic payment over the Internet, the traders need cryptographic protection. Since they never met before, they only came together for the deal, they had no shared key. For a time, this key issue was considered an insurmountable obstacle for free e-commerce. Not so, a young computer scientist, by the name of Ralph Merkle offered the first intellectual breakthrough for this challenge; Diffie and Hellman improved on it, and the RSA "gang" (Rivest, Shamir, and Adelman) followed suit. They established solutions based on two different keys, one private and one public. These methods are based on the assumed complexity for deducing the private key from the public one. Since the private/public key form a tight couple, it is mathematically necessary to be able to deduce one from the other, and the only question is how difficult – complex – would that be. The RSA cipher was used as a foundation for a US law regarding legal commitments through digital signatures. When a day will come and RSA will be compromised, (perhaps that day is here, who knows?) all the signed documents based on it, instantly will become questionable.

We have no alternative to the public/private key solution for any secret and confidential communication and payment between strangers. Apart from RSA, we have ECC and a handful of others, but no principled alternative exists, so we have no choice but to resort to these tools. Technically Ralph Merkle solution is different, as elaborated in chapter 4.

When the vision of digital money came to the fore, the solution approach to this challenge gravitated toward these amazing public/private key tools. *Are we on the right track?*

THE QUANTUM THREAT

After decades of following the blueprint offered by Alan Turing in 1936, computer science appears finally to breakthrough to a new type of computing device. The idea is to exploit nature's ability to resolve complexity in a parallel mode. Alan Turing constructed a sequential machine that handles complexity by stretching it out into linear, sequential, simple steps. Over the years, the speed of running through these sequences of steps was greatly improved, but the sequential paradigm was left unchanged. All the while, nature seems to resolve complexity in much more efficient ways. If you hold an 18 in. necklace by its ends such that the distance between them is 16 in., then the necklace instantly curves. The curvature is determined by the parts of the necklace, as they obey the law of gravity and the other Newtonian laws of mechanics. It will take some serious calculations for an Alan Turing computer to compute the exact curvature of the necklace. Yet, the necklace itself resolves this computational challenge instantly. And when you push your holding fingers closer, the curvature instantly adjusts. Clearly, the means used by nature to compute at any configuration the curvature of the necklace are different and more efficient than the Turing proposition. Pioneers, like Richard Feynman and Peter Shor have proposed a concrete way to use the quantum mechanical attributes of nature as a means to replace the sequential treatment of complexity with parallel strategy. Applied to cryptography, such a quantum computing machine will be able to simultaneously (rather than sequentially) examine all possible keys to crack a ciphertext, and spot the right key almost instantly. Early 2015, quantum computers still face a host of construction problems. Yet, the theoretical grounds are well established. Quantum computing will very likely defeat the complexity used in all mainstay ciphers. Erosive complexity may no longer serve as a viable basis for security, confidentiality, and privacy. This threat may materialize any day now. *It sure does not seem a good time to load all our money onto a vault fortified by erosive complexity.*

THE SECURITY ADVANTAGE OF DIGITAL CURRENCY

Crypto money is secured by cryptographic means. Cryptography is deemed the domain of complex math, and as everybody knows, math anchors its conclusions on unshakable grounds. So, one figures out that crypto money is immunized against hackers and thieves. Alas, as we have discussed above, modern cryptography is based on a fuzzy concept called intractability: a measure of how difficult would it be for an adversary to accomplish a computational task. The ancient Greeks were sweating on an intractable problem: trisecting an angle with a straightedge and a compass. Bisecting an angle was easy, but trisecting was resisting all attempts to accomplish it: it was declared "intractable." Eventually, more than a millennia later Pierre Wantzel (Cajori, 1918) proved the impossibility of doing so. The problem graduated from intractable to impossible. A simpler example is represented via the attempts to move about 31 domino pieces placed on a chess board, such that each domino piece covers two adjacent squares on the board. This leaves two squares uncovered, and allows for the pieces to move about. The goal is to move the pieces such that the uncovered squares will be the squares that share one of the two major diagonals on the board. People have been spending hours shoving and pushing the chess pieces here and there, finding it intractable to achieve the objective. A simple mathematical analysis would prove it to be impossible because each domino piece covers one white square and one black square, so the two uncovered squares must be of opposite colors, and can't share a diagonal. This too graduates a problem from intractable to impossible.

The reason that digital money security is a monster is that cryptographic intractability, has NOT GRADUATED to "impossibility." As many find surprising and quite unsettling, we have mathematical proofs that the cryptographic intractability that we rely on, for digital money and secure communication, is definitely and indisputably not impossible, but rather very possible. So, no mathematical grade assurance, sorry. By and large modern cryptography relies on erosive intractability, and no one can credibly predict how fast it would erode.

When it comes to secure communication such erosive intractability is a threat to watch, but not to panic about because if a given cipher loses its intractability (owing to faster computers, or deeper mathematical insight) then a replacement cipher will take over from that point on. But as far as money is concerned, losing the underlying mathematical intractability will amount to a catastrophic collapse, and a total blowout. This is a nightmare!

When we talk about digital money in this book, we talk about money form that is robust enough to handle micro- and nanopayments, as well as global and mega payment. In fact, we must allow for the digital format to conveniently handle the sum of the wealth of humanity. And we surely don't wish to wake up one day and find that a teen blogger published an algorithm to crack the money that the world is using.

With these notes about scope and range, and the reality of the security nightmare, we are prepared to sink our teeth into the challenge of providing reliable security for the new form of money: digital.

Currency stripped of its physicality, and fully expressed via a string of bits faces an acute risk of counterfeit. Let's consider Alice and Bob, two residents in cyber space. They wish to exercise a financial transaction between them – without involving a third party. Alice then is forwarding a 100 bits string, s, to Bob, claiming it to be a $1000 transaction. Bob needs to decide if s is real money, or not. In order to reach this decision Bob can (1) examine the string s and (2) request more "bits" from Alice. Suppose now Alice responds to Bob by forwarding a "proving" string p, designed to satisfy Bob that the transaction is all right. Consequently, Bob has two strings s and p to examine – but nothing more.

This would be simple for Bob to decide if he were the mint of that type of digital money. Bob (being the mint) was the one who composed the string s and then gave it to Carla against Carla paying him $1000. So now when the same string comes back to him he is sure that (1) it is worth $1000 and (2) this string was not claimed before (Bob keeps a ledger of all the coins he has redeemed). Bob would have no idea if Alice stole the money (string, s) from Carla, or Carla paid her with that string, for some services, or that perhaps Carla passed the money string to David, who passed it to Eve, on and on, until Alice got a hold of it, and now redeems it. If Alice stole the money then somewhere there is a victim, but it is not Bob. This is an important conclusion since Bob in our case is the one who takes the risk, sends out IOU notes that can come back and bankrupt him. His ledger will keep him financially immunized.

However, in the general case, where Bob is not the mint, just a regular trader, he is then totally clueless, as to the validity of s, and must decide on accepting or rejecting s as payment based solely on the bit contents of s and p.

Bob will attempt to use a decision algorithm, D, to make his decision. D will decide whether it is "good money" (G), or "fraudulent" (F). Let s contain $|s| = s$ bits, let there be g good (G) strings, and let there be f fraudulent (F) strings, then we have: $g + f = 2^s$. It is easy to conclude that the number of good string, g, cannot be very small, since then there will be no means to express all the necessary coins. Similarly g cannot be very large because in that case, it will be easy for Alice to put together a fake string that fools D. Now D should be a very fast and effective decision algorithm since the transaction must be carried out lightning fast. But, a fast D means that Alice could randomly try many different strings comprised of s bits, and check each of them with D, until she finds a string that D decrees as valid and good money. Alice will then forward that string to Bob, fooling him to accept it.

This analysis proves that the desired situation where Alice and Bob transact with digital money in cyber space and conclude their transaction without resorting to a third party or an external means, is not achievable. Resigned to this conclusion, let's see what type of external means can be used. Clearly an external "Oracle" will be helpful. Oracle in this context will be defined as an agent, an entity, with detailed knowledge of all the digital coins minted in this space, and their disposition at any moment. Bob will inquire from such an oracle whether the string s that Alice sent him is bona fide, or not. This reliance on an oracle will insure that any and all attempts by Alice to defraud Bob will be fertile, provided Alice does not manage to stand in for the oracle and fake its answers. And indeed, this simple solution is employed by all the various digital currencies on the market today. The traditional digital currencies (the centralized ones) rely on an oracle in the form of a database managed by the mint of that currency, and the new bitcoin-type currencies rely on a public ledger that is managed by a network protocol. In both versions the oracle's answers insure against counterfeits.

The oracle solution suffers from a troubling weakness: the execution of the transaction remains in limbo as long as the oracle has not spoken. And in cyber space, the communication with the oracle depends on the underlying network. The universal information highway, the Internet, was designed with robust principles of survivability and adaptability to surprise disconnects and sudden overloads, and its performance is exemplary. Yet, on occasions, the Internet is slow, hubs slow down and queues pile up. Also, the success of the Internet, spurs its growth – and its complexity, inviting ever more persistently a surprise implosion on account of overbearing complexity. It is exactly in situations of such painful surprises that money has to flow, motivate people, and coordinate solution efforts. If all transactions are stalled when the oracle does not respond fast enough, then we have a fundamental problem in our hand. Remember, this issue is the same for self-anchored bitcoin type and for fiat money-extended, centralized, digital currencies. For the former, the oracle takes the form of a public ledger, and for the latter, the mint-controlled database.

This weakness, this dependence on an oracle response time, may be solved by deterrence: building an environment of inhibiting punishment and measured retribution. If Alice will realize that the price to be paid for cheating Bob is high and exacting, then she would think twice before sending Bob a bad money string. Then say that Alice and Bob may agree to carry out a digital money transaction without getting the blessing of an oracle, but checking with the oracle at some future time. Should the oracle declare the transaction a fraud, then Alice will sustain a painful punishment. The greater the punishment, the less the likelihood that Alice will defraud Bob. Or say, the proportion of payers who would blatantly make a payment with a bad money string will be lower and lower, as the punishment for that action will be higher and higher. This is a classic situation for insurance companies to move in, charge a small premium, and insure the payee communities against the few who would defraud them. That punishment should be well measured and enforceable. But once applied it will be very useful in situations like (1) occasional slow down of the network creating long wait times for transaction approvals and (2) temporary loss of the network, like in a natural catastrophe, or a man-made disaster.

Together, the oracle and the retribution scheme work hand in hand to facilitate a seamless solution to frictionless payment. Another means will be to minimize the chance for noncommunicating transaction approval oracle, by replacing the single oracle with hierarchy of sub-oracles that would be comprised of many network nodes, such that each node could function as an oracle and authenticate a transaction. So, if the main oracle is out of reach, there will be so many other addresses on the network, ready to dispense an authentication for any given transaction.

DETERRENCE

For deterrence to work, it should be effective – the cost of fraud should be inescapable and high. And who would execute the "punishment?" There are two options: (1) the trading community and (2) society at large.

The Trading Community

An effective authority of the digital money trading community will mark a trader who paid with bad bits, and ban him or her from further trading. Alas, wily traders could trade anonymously, or keep trading using a different account. It is therefore that the trading community will opt to establish a cumulative index of good conduct. Namely, an index that builds up slowly as a trader behaves properly, but it drops precipitously upon a single instance of fraud, or attempt of fraud, or serious misbehavior. The cumulative index may be linked to an exposed identity, or to a masked identity – it works in both cases.

For example, a digital mint invites traders to buy its digital coins, using a public key as their specific, yet masked identity. The real identity of the traders remains hidden. In the beginning all transactions will require the "blessing" of the mint (that runs the full ledger of all the transactions among the masked identities). But as time goes by, some active traders accumulate a "good standing" marker (index) certifying that they have traded so much money for so long and all in good behavior. Should trader Alice pass a digital coin, $x = \$50$ to Bob, she might add to it, her good standing index, say $I = 70/100$. Bob, verifying the index, might agree to accept Alice's coin (x) reasoning that Alice will not be stupid enough to defraud him of $50, and a day later lose her high good standing index. The logic is compelling: it would take Alice a long time of good trading to qualify again for a high behavior index. Bob might set the limit on, say, $60 in that case. But if Carla passed to Bob digital coin, $y = \$120$, Bob might agree to register it as bona fide transaction because Carla has proven to Bob that she earned a good standing index of 85/100. It is true that Carla, using a masked identity, could continue to trade with this mint, using a new masked identity, but that new identity will have a very low trading index and would not enjoy the benefits of fast trading (and other benefits) allotted to traders with high index of good standing. By and large, traders will not opt to trade with many masked entities because no such entity will be endowed with a high enough index to open the door for instant transactions without waiting for the mint's approval.

Naturally for a trading community where the mint insists on exposure of a trader's new identity in order to do business with the mint, the range of possible "punishment" for fraudsters is much greater. Exposed cheaters may be properly prosecuted the way the state prosecutes people who write bad checks. But the previous example shows so very clearly, that even without exposure of the traders' true identity, effective counter-action against fraudsters may be taken.

The measure of response to a fraud attempt may be calibrated to uproot, or minimize this avenue of fraud.

Deterrence Through Society at Large

In just about every state or society, the act of willful fraud by paying with bad money is considered a prosecutable crime. It is possible then to unleash the power of society at large upon the offenders. This can be readily done in the case where society keeps score of financial integrity and monetary behavior. Such markers are earned via a prolonged, consistent conduct of honesty, fairness, and integrity. A single incident of fraud or attempt of fraud by forwarding bad digits as good money will wipe out the integrity score that took the fraudsters years to build up. The principle then is like the case with the mint keeping integrity score. In the United States, there are three companies that keep "credit scores" for all Americans based on regular scanning of the public record. Americans are routinely checking their scores with Equifax, TransUnion, and Experian, worried that identity thieves have ruined their hard-earned high score. Originally, these scores were compiled to serve as risk mediators for banks deciding whether a loan applicant is a good risk. But, over time these scores have proven useful in real estate rental decision, for sifting through job applicants, and even for choices in the romantic arena. The more these scores are used by evaluators, the more do Americans care about them. If Alice has a poor credit score, she is out of luck. Bob, on the other hand has a high credit score. He can then buy from a credit rating company, a cryptographic certificate that identifies him by a unique number and asserts his credit score. When Bob is rushing through a retail store, buying a book, for $23.50, he forwards that amount in the form of a digital string of ones and zeros. Along with the money, Bob presents his certificate for good credit rating. The point of sale (POS) terminal at the store, will execute a short and fast dialog with Bob's phone. This dialog is a well-established cryptographic protocol that assures the vendor that the payer is the bona fide holder of the certificate. The vendor also records the identification number of the payer (a mask for the true identity of the buyer), and if the credit score is high enough, the vendor releases the book to Bob, without having to request, wait, and record a transaction approval code from the mint. In fact, the above-mentioned cryptographic dialog can be exercised between two devices, which are battery operated. This implies that such trust-based transactions may be carried out in dire situations where the network is down and cyberspace disappears. The idea here is that Bob, rational as he is expected to be, will not opt to steal the petite sum of $23.50 against losing his hard-earned high credit score. If Bob cheats, the vendor will so realize by the end of the day, when the vendor uploads the day's transactions to the digital mint. The vendor response would be to relay this fraud case to the credit rating company that issued Bob's certificate. By the unique id number reported by the vendor, the credit rating company would know who Bob is, and instantly kill his high credit rating – a lasting blow. Bob may have to wait some 7 years, according to current US law, before this cheating incident can be forgotten. The people who behave responsibly with money and earn a high credit score are very aware of its benefit, are thoughtful individuals, and very few, if any of them would choose to take up the cheating route. At any rate, plenty insurance companies will readily offer an inexpensive insurance to vendors, to make them whole, should they become victim to such a fraud.

It is noteworthy that paying by sending off a digital string is carried out via dedicated payment software that is built to insure against faking bits and double spending. This means that to cheat, it is necessary to be very proactive, negating any excuse that it all happened by mistake.

THE ORACLE

Having concluded that it is hopeless to search for a decision algorithm used by Bob to assure himself that a digital string claimed by Alice to be worth money is indeed so, we now retort to the presence of a knowledgeable source – an oracle – that is aware of all the minted coins, and their redemption status. This oracle will be able to assure Bob that he is being paid good money. The fundamental worry with this arrangement is the undisturbed availability of the oracle, and its ability to respond in real time, without a burdensome delay. We have today the experience of the payment card industry where transactions are authenticated in real time with a rather impressive record of performance. Yet, one must note that instances of unacceptable delay, temporary shut down, and even prolonged blackouts are also part of the record.

This connectivity problem is shared by self-anchored crypto money like bitcoin and its many imitators, and by any centralized currency minting digitized fiat money, like BitMint. In the first case, the oracle is maintained and managed by the community of the traders, and in the second case by the organizing mint.

The risk with this oracle solution is comprised of (1) fake oracle, (2) man-in-the-middle, (3) successful attack on the oracle, and (4) brute force attack.

Fake oracle: Bob may contact what appears to be the oracle, but in fact is a fraudster masquerading as the oracle. The fake oracle OKs the money, and Bob does not find out about it until he tries to pay that money further. Bitcoin came up with an elegant solution to this risk: the open-ledger that constitutes the oracle is constructed as many layers of cryptographic locks, which are believed to be very hard to crack or fake, while being very easy to verify. The bitcoin ledger, by its very appearance amounts to proof-of-work that could have been accomplished only by the network as a whole. It is too much to do all that work for any individual trader, or for any minority of collaborating fraudulent traders. The centralized mint, on the other hand, keeps its ledger confidential, and only submits a specific answer to the validity of a specific coin. Since the traders don't have visibility into the mint database, it is more likely that a fraudster will fake the mint, and dispense fake answers. This boils down to identity verification and is discussed in the section regarding transit security. There are various means to insure someone's identity, and since the identity of the mint is so crucial, it will justify even the more expensive and elaborate tools. A simple way for Bob to verify that he converses with the real, not a fake mint, is to send a coin in his possession, and ask the mint to report its validity and any tethering associated with it. A fake mint will be unable to handle this query, and will not even know if Bob's query is one for which he knows the answer, or not.

Man-in-the-middle: This risk relates to the following eventuality: Alice passes to Bob a fake digital coin, then she intercepts Bob's query to the mint, and sends to the mint the right coin (which she posses). The mint OK's the right coin, and so communicates back to Bob who innocently believes that the mint has just authenticated the coin he sent to it, and accepts the money. This risk is covered in the section about transit security. In addition, the protocol for high value coins may include the mint sending back the coin to Bob, encrypted with its private key. Another solution will call for the mint to exchange the valid queried coin with another just minted one. It is noteworthy that unlike the mint penetration risk, this one involves the payee, not the mint!

Successful attack on the mint: The bitcoin solution against faking the public ledger (the oracle) will be ever so effective against compromising the ledger. In both cases the cryptographic hurdles are widely considered insurmountable by any dishonest trader, or a minority group of dishonest traders. It is noteworthy that a majority of traders can do whatever they want to trump, and quash the rights and wealth of the trusting minority, since bitcoin's philosophy is based on the premise that the majority is wise, trustworthy, honest, and even courageous to stand against any evil and abusive minority. This premise is not guaranteed by any super power; it is simply the working hypothesis of the bitcoin "co-religionists." Similarly, the notion that the cryptographic work chain cannot be cracked is hinged on an unproven but widely believed premise. Anyone aware of how many times in history, widely believed premises were proven wrong, will not be so worry free while transforming his crown jewels to bitcoin, or its likes.

Unlike bitcoin, the mint has no such proof of work element in its defense, and it can indeed be compromised, causing it to OK fake money. Such eventuality will bring down the mint, and its money trade, and thus, this risk should receive very considerable thought.

Fortunately, there are several effective means to prevent the invasion of the mint coin database. While a reader might be rather skeptic in light of the very frequent instances where commercial and financial databases are routinely penetrated, this mint case is different. By and large, the penetrated databases have many bona fide visitors. These visitors keep their credentials in their home computers. All that a hacker has to do, is to find one bona fide visitor with a computer system managed by lesser quality security team – compromise this lower grade system, steal the visiting credentials in his target database, and use them to get in. The mint, by contrast, has no "bona fide" visitors. It does its own examination of the database, and provides a binary answer to a query regarding the validity of a binary string. Unlike many retail stores, the mint's heart and soul are in its cyber security, so full concentration is allocated to the security of its coin database.

The mint will use write-once technology for listing its digital coins, so that no hacker can change the digital signature of the managed coin. The mint is likely to keep the coin data encrypted. And since the risk for compromise and its damage is proportional to the value of the coin, and since also the mint could exact service fee proportional to the value of the coin, the mint will be financially well disposed to allocate security commensurate with the value of the minted coin. So high value coins could be kept in two or more separate and disjoint databases. Upon a query the multiple databases will decrypt their data, and all the results will be compared. If any database differs from the rest, this will serve as an alarm for something gone wrong.

Brute force attack: Alice has a nonzero chance to correctly guess the bit composition of a coin. When Bob checks the coin with the mint, it gets the "green light," but when Bob later on attempts to redeem it, it is being rejected as having been redeemed already by its rightful owner. Bob then will have a valid claim against the mint, for having misled him. This risk could be averted by exchanging the queried coin against a same value newly minted one. Only in that case, the valid owner of the coin would not be able to redeem it. It is clear that a successful guess of the bit composition of a coin is very bad news.

The best strategy to scuttle and scotch this threat is to mint entropic digital coins, of which there are other important advantages.

ENTROPIC COINS

Given a digital coin defined via a string (s), which is n bits long, the irreducible chance for an attacker to correctly guess the identity of the n bits is $p_s = 2^{-n}$. This low limit will be the real chance only if s is fully random. Any manifest bit pattern will pump the chance higher, with no lower limit than $p_s = 1.00$. This fact can be expressed using the notion of entropy as devised by Claude Shannon. Shannon defined information entropy $H = -\sum p_i \log(p_i)$ for $i = 1, 2, \ldots 2^n$, where p_i is the chance to correctly guess the identity of string i, one particular n-bits string among the distinct 2^n options. If s is "fully patterned," fully predictable, then the entropy is $H = H_{min} = 0$, and when s is fully randomized, and each string has the same value of $p_i = 2^{-n}$ to be the right guess, then $H = H_{max} = n$. The greater the pattern in s, the closer the entropy shifts to H_{min}, and the farther from H_{max}. The lower the entropy, the greater the chance of an assailant to guess the makeup of the coin, and defraud the mint and its traders.

Clearly, then the mint will strive to remove any pattern from its digital coins. Ideally, the mint will construct its coins from purely random bits, or at least from a strong pseudorandom bit generator. It would appear though that some pattern in the bit structure is unavoidable since the coin must carry both identity and value. And the value must be interwoven into the identity expression in order to fuse the two and enable the all-important tethering.

To elaborate: suppose the mint will construct its coins from n purely randomized bits that would spell out the identity of the coin, and then concatenate it with m bits that would be interpreted as the value of the coin, say, $10. Well, then, a wily counterfeiter will be able to replace the m value bits with another string m' that would read: $1000, and claim that the coin comprised of $n + m'$ bits represents $1000, not $10. Encrypting n and m together will not be of much help because the two parts are then subject to reverse encryption.

To foil this scheme it is necessary for the mint to interweave the identity with the value of the coin, but by doing so, it infuses pattern (value reading) into the coin, and thereby suppresses its guessing entropy.

This dilemma may be solved by removing the value information from the identities of the bits. By doing so, it would be possible to dedicate the bit identities to the definition of the identity of the coin, namely to pick the identity of each of the n bits in a completely random fashion. So, how will one indicate value? Other than the identities of the string bits there is only one data element associated with the string, and that is its size, or its bit count, n. By devising a value function $v(coin) = v(n)$, the mint will assign a value to the coin, all the while keeping the identities of the bits in a purely random fashion (highest guessing entropy, the most difficult string to guess).

Looking further into this solution one finds additional attractions: the value function v may be constructed to satisfy: $v(r \times n) = r \times v(n)$, where $0 \leq r \leq 1$, which will allow a coin holder to split his coin, and pay a fraction thereof. Example: a digital coin, s, is comprised of $n = 200$ bits. The bits are randomly assigned, so that the guessing chance of the coin is an infinitesimal: $p_s = 1/2^{200} = 1/1.60 \times 10^{60}$. The coin value is computed via $v = 0.25 \times n$, namely, $v = 0.25 \times 200 = 50$. Alice who owns the coin ($coin_{Alice}$) wishes to pay $20 to Bob, ($coin_{bob}$), and keep the balance of $30 to herself ($coin_{change}$). She would then divide the 200 bits coin to the first 120 bits valued: $v = 0.25 \times 120 = 30$, and the complementing 80 bits valued: $v = 0.25 \times 80 = \$20$. Alice will then send Bob the latter 80 bits, which a hacker will face, a guessing chance of $p_{Bob-coin} = 1/2^{80} = 1/1.21 \times 10^{24}$, and keep the change coin with herself. In other words, Alice accomplished coin splitting without consulting the mint. This advantage is of fundamental value for all sorts of pay-as-you-go regimen, like paying for parking time, or paying real time for consumed electrical power, or burning gas. It is of great value for micro- and nanopayments. And since the mint has full freedom to determine v, it can assure that even a small denomination will be expressed through sufficient number of bits to insure a comfortably high guessing entropy.

These fully randomized coins – entropic coins – offer another important advantage: they foil the most universal tool of cryptanalysis, brute force. A hacker who captured a ciphertext produced by a known method will simply try to decrypt it with all the possible keys until finding the one key that would decrypt the ciphertext to a plausible plaintext. All the major ciphers in use today will succumb to this attack, hopefully after a long time when the cracking will no longer be useful for the cracker. But an entropic coin will decrypt to a random looking bit sequence when the wrong key is used and also when the right key is used – no difference, so the attacker will have no knowledge, no feedback as to whether a key he tried is the right key or not. And that frustration will apply regardless of the cipher used to encrypt the coin.

Another most powerful and helpful attribute of the entropic coins is its informative masking.

ENTROPIC COINS: INFORMATIVE MASKING

An entropic coin like in the previous example, comprised of 200 bits is so well defended against a guessing attack that, as we have seen one could reduce the number of identity defining bits to say only 100 bits. The guessing chance will still be infinitesimal: $1/2^{100} = 1/1.27 \times 10^{30}$. Say then, the mint could mask the bit identity of 100 bits out of the 200 bits of the coin, and still trade with a highly secure coin.

Let's first define a masking language: we shall use 2 bits to identify each coin bit. Namely, a 200 bits coin will be stated with 400 bits. The masking language will be defined as follows: a coin bit marked "0" will be expressed as a double zero "00", and a coin bit marked "1" will be expressed via two bits, "11". The combination "01" will serve to mark the beginning of the coin string, and the combination "10" will mark the end of the string. Namely, a 10 bits coin identified as 1101101110 will be written as 01 11 11 00 11 11 00 11 11 11 00 10. Now suppose the mint wishes to mask the identity of bit 3, so the coin now looks: 11?1101110. Using our masking language it will look: 01 11 11 01 11 11 00 11 11 11 00 10. Bit three which was written before as "00" is now written as "01". We use the string-start combination "01" to indicate a bit with masked identity. All combinations "01" within the coin will be interpreted as masked bits because this combination will mark a string start only after one encounters a string end "10". So, if the mint masks the identities of bits 2, 3, 5, and 6 (coin = 1??1??1110), then it would be written as: 01 11 01 01 11 01 01 11 11 11 00 10.

Using the bit masking language the mint could pass along the 200 bits coin with 100 bits masked. And in due course redeem that very coin to a redeemer that presents the right identity of the 100 bits with the disclosed identity. What is the advantage of this exercise? There are $C_{200}^{100} = 9.05 \times 10^{58}$ combinations to pick 100 masked bits from a 200 bits coin. This means that by choosing a specific combination of 100 bits to mask the mint one can imprint on the coin a message selected from a huge message dictionary, containing about 10^{59} messages. And the mint could also decide to mask 99 bits, which can be selected in 8.96×10^{58} ways, and decide to mask 98, 97, or 96 bits with selection options: 8.70×10^{58}, 8.27×10^{58}, or 7.72×10^{58}, respectively, and so on and so forth. All this amounts to a very large message space that can be attached to each minted coin. This messaging option can be used to identify use of the coin (tethering), identify whom the coin was minted for, etc.

Bit masking may be used iteratively: the mint might mask, say 10 bits out of the 200 (there are 2.24×10^{16} ways to do so) and pass the coin to Alice. Alice in turn will mask 10 additional bits from the 190 unmasked bits (there are 1.327×10^{16} ways to do it), and pass it to Bob. Bob will mask some bits of his choice, and so on, each adding information to the traded coin. Of course, this encoding will have to make sure that (1) the number of unmasked bits left at the point of redemption would be sufficiently high – with high enough entropy – to keep the chance of successful guessing negligible; and (2) that no masking step will result in a confusion between two coins that differ from each other only in the identities of the masked bits.

One practical application for bit masking is in implementing a network of sub-oracles. If the main oracle shares the full measure of coin data with a large number of sub-oracles, then the risk mounts for someone working for a sub-oracle unit to aim to defraud the mint by using coin information given to that sub-oracle. The corrupt individual will approach the mint from another sub-oracle, or through the main oracle itself, forward the coin data, and demand its redemption. The mint will do so because everything checks out. Only that at some point, the bona fide owner of this coin will be unable to redeem it because it was already redeemed. To prevent this likely eventuality (especially with a wide network of sub-oracles), the main oracle could mask some bits from every coin it passes the data to a sub-oracle. The unmasked bits will be of sufficient count to credibly allow the sub-oracle to validate a redeemer claim for the coin, but the missing masked bits will not allow anyone working for the sub-oracle to turn around and claim the coin via a different sub-oracle. By choosing a different set of bits to mask, the oracle will be able to insure that even a group of corrupt individuals working at different sub-oracles will not together have enough information to defraud the mint. The mint will choose different bits to mask, for every sub-oracle, in order to keep track of where a fraud attempt came from.

THE SUB-ORACLE

We noted above that the oracle solution to OK each and every transaction poses a tall order: uninterrupted availability and instant response ability. This requirement can be honored most of the time, but not all the time. We discussed the deterrence method as one way to help out with such failing network instances, and in this section we present another solution. It is based on an entity called the sub-oracle.

Suppose we wish to alleviate the burden from the oracle, by cloning it. Having now oracle-1 and oracle-2, we have a greater degree of freedom to use one or the other for any coin query we may have. While it is enticing we may soon realize that the two oracles will have to synchronize constantly, otherwise Alice could pass the same coin once to Bob who would verify it on oracle-1, and once to Carla who would verify it on oracle-2. Yet, we may notice that cloning the oracle, even many times, will work fine against fake money. The problem is limited to double spending. Alternatively, we may divide the database to two parts, and give priority for the first part of the database to oracle-1 while allocating priority for the second part to oracle-2. There is 50% chance that a query will be addressed to the oracle which has priority on it and 50% of the queries will have to sustain a short wait time while the queried oracle queries the other one which has priority over this coin. This presents a performance challenge: to arrange the clones such that queries will be directed to the right clone (with priority over that coin), at high probability. Should there be 10 oracle clones, each "owning" 10% of the coins, while the likelihood that the owner clone will be queried is higher than 10%, then the configuration design of the clone is effective. Such clones, that are each in some way less than the original oracle, are referred to as sub-oracles.

For example, Alice buys a $400 digital coin from a digital mint that recognizes Alice as living in proximity to a big shopping mall. The mint will then pass the data about these $400 to the sub-oracle associated with that shopping mall. Chances are that Alice frequents this mall regularly and will spend there most of the $400 digital coins. The receiving merchant in the mall will naturally query the mall sub-oracle, and get a local answer right away.

TRANSIT SECURITY

Underneath the issue of counterfeit money, we find the issue of in-transit fraud: the digital coin sent from Alice to Bob is hijacked by Harry the hacker, who rushes to redeem it. Alternatively, Harry poses as Bob, fools Alice with his stolen identity, then redeems the coin.

This challenge is not unique to payment, and there are several well-established tools to meet it. These are tools for: (1) encryption and (2) identity verification. We have discussed earlier the advantage of entropic coins – they resist a brute force attack. As to identity verification, there are many tools that may be used in conjunction with the associated risk. Some digital transactions may be conducted between strangers who remain strangers after the transaction, meaning there is nothing to verify. This may happen when Alice sells Bob a song, and the digital version of the song streams from Alice to whoever is counter-streaming to her the price of the song in a digital format. All that Alice will insure is that the song is streaming down to the one who is sending her the money in counter-parallel mode.

When a coin is tethered to Alice, then the mint is obligated to exercise an agreed upon identity verification protocol to authenticate that it is Alice who attempts to redeem it. The robustness of the protocol may be commensurate with the value of the coin. Simple verification scheme may rely on proving identity with a secret code; others would use two or more codes and passwords; and yet another identity verification protocol will use a second device, for instance a code sent over a phone, or require some smart dialog that only the true identity would know how to handle. Protocols may be based on biometrics, E.g.: fingerprints, eye iris, palm structure etc.

INTERMINT SECURITY

The Intermint, a network of digital money mints, mentioned earlier, also contributes to the security of the digital money transactions. The Intermint protocol will impose a quick separation and disengagement of the healthy mints from any infected and compromised ones, so that in the unlikely event, of a bank compromise, the integrity of the trading environment will stay intact.

TIGHTENING THE DEFENSE PERIMETER

Today hackers can and do steal money from any bank and financial institution where money is kept and accounted for. The method is simple in concept: the hackers exploit the fact that most financial institutions use one of very few choices for machine (hardware), operating system (software), and applications (software). By studying these few options the hackers bring to bear a sophisticated planning scheme designed to pass unnoticed through the least alert minds of the people hired to provide cyber security. In February 2015, the headlines were screaming about multiple bank theft in the past few months, with estimated value of one billion dollar, perhaps more. The victims are highly regarded well-secured major international banks. If one draws a line around the hundred of thousands of financial institutions from where the hackers may start their penetration journey, then one will draw a very long battle line. This large front poses a very tempting and potent opportunity for the hackers who simply probe and test various banks and financial institutions until they find one with a weakness, and a vulnerability, and get in through there. The banks and the financial institutions are all linked, so getting through to one loose security financial institution will serve as an opening to many more banks and theft targets.

Using tethered digital money, the stored money in the bank will be cryptographically linked to its rightful owner, and theft of that money will offer no benefit to the thief who will be unable to redeem it. The "victim," on his part, will be readily compensated – that what tethering to owner is all about. In a tethered digital money regimen many banks, merchants, and individuals holding vast amounts of money, all keep their money assets as redeemable only by the assigned owner. So a thief will be unable to redeem it. This in turn, shrinks the now long perimeter of attack, to a tight and narrow front line strictly around the mint. The integrity of the entire trading environment is based on the integrity of the mint. The best and brightest security people will be focused on securing this narrow front line. The security team will force the assailants to come to their security turf, and fight it out there with a clear advantage to the white hat team.

DIGITAL CURRENCY: THE COMPLEXITY ROUTE

Captivated by the elegance of public/private key schemes, the pioneers of digital money from the now defunct, still brilliant DigiCash to the still humming, globally challenging, bitcoin, have all relied on this solution approach to constitute a digital money offering. Some digital money solutions are very humble, designed for small amounts to be used as micropayments and such. These solutions are not very important for our interest here. Our attention is for a digital money solution that is robust enough to carry unlimited amounts of money, in a rich variety of fast-pace transactions and provide security, integrity, and accountability.

Let's assume we have such a system and we are happy with it. The public calls it "Easy Gold." The convenience of digital money gradually sucks most of the monetary assets of humanity into this digital format. Easy to store, easy to move, easy to account, safe, secure – virtual perfection. Easy Gold lasts 1, 2, or 10 years, until we forget about paper bills, old-fashioned coins and gold bars.

And then one day, an unknown math professor from a little known dictatorship had an idea. Inspired by the Laplace transform that resolves complexity by representing a problem on a different domain, this professor finds a quick way to deduce the private key from the public key. He makes the mistake and shares his finding with his boss. The professor disappears the next week, and over time, persistent rumors emerge regarding mysterious financial resources exercised by this tiny dictatorship. A year later a prodigy in Rome discovers pretty much the same shortcut, and publishes it on his Facebook page. Some are quick to realize what this shortcut means, they use the trick to create fake money out of thin air, and quickly dispose of it in a shopping splurge. Within four weeks from its publication, the international monetary system is completely dysfunctional. No one accepts "Easy Gold" any longer, and all fortunes denominated in "Easy Gold" become worthless. The years of joy riding on "Easy Gold," international easy payment and the universal rich-parade, have come to a screeching halt. People dig for their old coins.

This imaginary scenario represents one of many possible ways in which a monetary system that hinges on *assumed (unproven) complexity* is fundamentally vulnerable to a future mathematical insight that would melt this complexity away. The most successful digital money to date is bitcoin, based on public/ private key complexity. Bitcoin was invented in a published article undersigned "Satoshi Nakamoto." The article exhibits good command of modern cryptography. Alas, no one seems to know a person by that name. The community of public domain cryptographers is small, and closed knit, yet there is not even a credible suspicion for who Mr Nakamoto may be. Like every oddity, especially in crypto stuff, this fact springs rumors, mostly unsubstantiated, as far as I can tell. One interesting rumor suggests that this digital money solution is a ruse of a powerful foreign government, who is hoping that more and more people will use it, since this government knows how to break the code and steer the money or fake it to its advantage.

The argument here is not against bitcoin in particular, but against the solution approach that attempts to extrapolate crypto tools used for transient communication and apply them to express money in a reliable, credible, stable, and robust way. Complexity may look stable and durable, but it has been shown through the history of science that complexity melts away before the power of superior intelligence and before the crashing force of persistent, aggressive innovation efforts. Money, by its very nature, always attracted the most brilliant robbers and thieves, who applied very persistent innovation in going after it. Today's bad guys will do the same. We should be cautious enough not to give them the opportunity. Let us not relax with a false sense of arrogance and hubris. Bad guys may have good brains; they are surely highly motivated. Even if we are thoroughly impressed with the patent complexity of our digital money solution, let us break the chain of repeating mistakes. The boundary between confidence and overconfidence is quite murky; let's not go near there. *Complexity shielded digital currency is a nonstarter.*

Modern science developed a flaring love affair with the tantalizing notion of complexity. All of a sudden, complexity is the most admired, most mystic-laden, most wondrous construct of life and nature. After all, scientists argue the formation of human kind is a product of complexity done right. The nonhierarchical Internet is a marvel of self-organized complexity. The marketplace, the stock market – all examples of complexity, showcase results that could not have been duplicated through a command performance.

The collapse of the Soviet Union at the feet of capitalism is regarded by many as an immutable proof that hierarchies are passé, command is narrow, and wisdom and prosperity are the domain of the head-less interactive system that is known as complexity. Mathematical models have proven that a bunch of simple-minded "beings" who can pass their lessons from one generation to the next, are capable of adapting to harsh realities, survive under oppressive conditions, and prosper into realms unforeseen by the components of this complexity.

Indeed, in complexity the whole is not simply an accounting sum of its parts – it is an entity that is not a mere size adjustment of its subset. A Shakespearian play is not a dictionary list of the words used, a Monet painting is not a table of which pigments were brushed on the canvass, and our consciousness as human beings is surely not encompassed in the chemical ingredients that our body is composed of.

Money is a complex system *par excellence*. Money works by it being distributed throughout society. And as society becomes globally integrated, it naturally evolves into shared currencies and into a mutual ability to make payment across town and across the globe. Each member of society: individual, organization, corporation, and government is an independent agent, deciding each on its own, where and how to make and spend money. The complexity of all of us should guarantee our survival and prosperity because we will adapt, invent, and grow.

Indeed, only that complexities grow in a process known as "trial and error" and every so often the error is so big that the complexity collapses, and then the remnants regroup and retry. And what is more – the larger the size of the complex system, the greater the chance for a pending devastating collapse. The dinosaurs ruled the earth and were best skilled to adapt to earth changes. Our ancestors, the mammals, were second fiddle. But then a cosmic event, a falling meteorite, changed the prevailing conditions, the world as it was before died off, and our ancestors moved up. We have seen empires grow, implode, and being replaced by new powers. Our financial history is punctuated by devastating recessions and depressions, with millions losing their life savings. And all that happened when the systems were not nearly as big, not remotely as integrated, not functionally so fast, so immediate, so responsive, as they are today. We don't yet have the science to predict when, but we know enough to realize that a big one is coming.

But we ignore it because life is so smooth and effective when all shines, when stability seems to rule, when we pay by phone, bank online, and treat the cloud as our pocket asset. The people who build these integrated systems surely wish for people to use them, and use them much. They have no interest to scare us, and keep us backward with yesterday's technology; they vie for a handsome return on their investment.

And when we contemplate reshaping money into digital format, and changing monetary reality with tethered money, it is incumbent upon us to consider the lurking danger of a complexity blowout.

We would like to develop some metrics that would alert us to a pending calamity. We would also like to develop some means to prevent a teetering system collapse and means to alleviate an avalanche as it rages. And finally, we would wish to have some means to recover from a tsunami that left our former shining complexity as a heap of debris.

Signs of a pending blow are discernable in the money exchange, so we need to insure maximum transaction visibility with our tethered digital money. One clear way to prevent a blow and to alleviate one is to slow down the exchange rate. We would like to have this ability, but to do that we need a system that would not be totally devoid of hierarchical attributes. We do wish to have some central control, but not to the extent that the lively powers of complexity are asphyxiated.

Another tool that we might consider for handling this challenge is the built-in ability for a quick disengagement. Meaning – while we wish to function as one large global system – seamlessly connecting each of the seven billion of us to one another – we also wish to have "break up lines" that in an emergency we can use to break up our large system into smaller independent systems, that are self sustaining and can work (not with the full capability of integrated system) and function until the storm is over.

Finally, for recovery, we need to be able to *remint money, redistribute money*, and in the case of a complete wipeout of our tenets and precepts, start all over again. And maybe we could use a temporary currency to help us through a tough transition period.

These requirements are quite tough. Bitcoin and other contenders don't seem to meet this standard.

DURABLE CRYPTOGRAPHY

While it is true that all mainstay cipher systems in use today are based on erosive complexity, it is also true that nonerosive cryptography does exist, and is in a position to claim its service. One category of durable crypto is very old, and one is very new. As early as 1917, Gilbert S. Vernam, an American engineer with Bell Labs registered a crypto patent: "The Vernam Cipher." It was, and still is, an unbreakable encryption system. Ironically, it was used by Stalin's spies as they stole the US Atomic bomb secrets, and these communications can't be read by the NSA to this very day. Gilbert Vernam has not resorted to erosive complexity, but rather applied the principle of *equivocation*. When a cryptanalyst tries to crack a Vernam ciphertext and spot the hidden plaintext, he is soon hit by a daunting surprise. While in a normal erosive complexity cipher, it is very difficult to spot the sought-after plaintext because every cracking attempt (except one) yields a bad answer; with Vernam, it is the opposite: many cracking attempts yield a good answer. Meaning, there are many possible and plausible plaintext options that could each encrypt into *the same given ciphertext*. And the crux of the problem (for the cryptanalyst) is that there is no mathematical way to reduce this large list of possible, and plausible plaintext options. Clearly, the ciphertext encrypts only one from the list of possible and plausible, but which? If we catch an enemy communication and when we try to decrypt it we find that "We shall attack after dawn" is a possible and plausible plaintext corresponding to the intercepted ciphertext, but the message "We shall attack before dawn" is also a possible plaintext for the same ciphertext, and to add insult to injury the message "We shall not attack at all" is a third possibility, and if we have no way to sort out these options, then – we have got nothing, do we? We are not the wiser by virtue of catching the ciphertext and exploring its possible plaintexts. It is not complexity that daunts us – it was not hard to extract these plausible options – it is rather equivocation that stands between the cryptanalyst and his goal. Only one of these options was the one that was encrypted, but without the key we don't know which. And this ignorance is solid and durable. It does not erode or wash away.

So why don't we all use durable equivocation instead of erosive complexity?

The story here is a classic example of the principle of Knowledge Realization Momentum (KRM).[4] When Mr Vernam patented his equivocation-based cipher, the only people who used cryptography were spooks and spies. And these characters had to memorize the key as they penetrated enemy territory. Alas, Vernam cipher demanded a new key to encrypt a new message, and what's more – the key has to be as long as the encrypted message. So, while his cipher was undoubtedly unbreakable, it was also undoubtedly impractical. Crypto science moved toward short, easy to memorize, and reusable keys. And that trend created a knowledge realization momentum that continues until today. Even though today keys are conveniently stored in large memory banks, and using a fresh key for every new message is quite doable. A few maverick cryptographers have come to resurrect and revive this old thrown-away concept. One such revival is captured in the Daniel cipher (see Appendix) which features a key of at-will size. Daniel is functioning as an erosive-complexity cipher when used with small keys, but it gradually transforms into an equivocation cipher when larger keys are used. This attribute points to Daniel as a fitting tool for digital money.

Another prospect for durable cryptography is emerging in the form of a quantum computer. The novel idea here is that data in a quantum state is sensitive to reading. Normally, if Alice reads a book before passing it to Bob, then Bob will have no sign in the words of the book that Alice read through it (unless Alice left some coffee stains ...). The data on the book is unaffected by it being read once, or as many times as one tries. But if data can be written into an unstable state (quantum state) then reading it will stabilize it, and hence leave a taletell sign. Think of a coin turning around on a hard surface. To read it as "head" or "tail," one must stop its turning, and hence signal that reading took place. For cryptography, this means that if data was accessed by a hacker, it would show. This, so the theory goes, will make quantum cryptography durable. When the time comes and quantum computing becomes operational, this principle will be put to its field test.

---

4. The principle of Knowledge Realization Momentum states that we extract new knowledge within topics, which were productive earlier, and overlook new knowledge waiting for us within topics that have not yielded new knowledge earlier. See G. Samid "Knowledge Realization Momentum–The Subtle Trap of Unidirectional Innovation" Int'l Conf. Information and Knowledge Engineering I IKE'11 I.

Chapter 4

Anatomy of Digital Money Products

Chapter Outline

So far in this book, we referred to money expressed as a digital string – digital money – in a generic form. Somehow we treat a series of ones and zeros as money. In this chapter we will examine the various ideas about how to do that – how to credibly assign a monetary value to something that reads like: 100001000111101101...

THEORY AND DEFINITION OF DIGITAL COINS

A digital coin is an entity that amounts to a string of bits (ordered bits, $\{0,1\}$). This string must have a numeric value, and must have an identity. The first requirement is obvious: a coin associated with no value is not a coin at all. The

Tethered Money: Managing Digital Currency Transactions. http://dx.doi.org/10.1016/B978-0-12-803477-4.00004-1

second requirement is posted in order to prevent double spending. Coins with a definite physical existence are inherently immunized against double spending: once paid, the physical coin changes hands, and the original payer can hardly pay this coin again. But a digital coin keeps a copy of itself in the hands of the payer, who can repay with the same. The only way to prevent this unacceptable situation is to assign a definite, unique, identity to each coin, such that if the very same coin is used by Alice to pay Bob, and also to pay Carla, then some intercepting mechanism will have a chance to catch this deception. Without a unique identity, there is no chance to ascertain the fraud of double spending.

We may further infer that when Alice passes a coin to Bob, Bob has no way to insure that Alice has not paid the very same coin to Carla beforehand. Whatever inspection Bob may desire over the digital coin, and over any subsequent dialogue with Alice, could have produced an identical result if Alice previously passed the coin to Carla. Hence double spending must be prevented via an "oracle" – a third party that has visibility over the set of coins in circulation. We will see that the oracle is a central mint, for centralized currency, and a public ledger for decentralized currencies. We also may conclude that any decision algorithm D devised by Bob to determine the validity of Alice's coin could be fooled by Alice through sufficient trials and errors. So, validity too has to be handled by an "oracle."

Looking ahead, we face a revolutionary new data technology based on quantum mechanics. Quantum data, by contrast to ordinary data, is changed upon observation. In other words, every "look" at the data leaves "finger prints" that testify that this "looking" happened. Once this technology matures, this could serve as a basis to foil double spending, but the need for coin identity will still be valid.

What is left is the threat of a successful guessing of the coin bits. A cyber thief may guess the bits of a valid coin that has not been double spent, and inform the oracle that this coin, which is legally owned by Alice, has now been transferred to the thief. (Alice would not know about this theft in real time, but the oracle will not realize it in time either.) The guessing threat is serious because it can be tried time and again. If a hacker guesses wrong, he cannot be prevented from trying again, because it may be that the rightful owner is trying to redeem it now. And so the only way to handle this threat is to make the likelihood of guessing sufficiently low to withstand countless guessing attempts.

The best strategy to prevent guessing is to use perfectly randomized coins, but imperfectly randomized coins are effective too.

Randomized Coins

In theoretical terms, the way to reduce the chance of deceitful guessing is to increase the entropy of the string. Entropy is an arbitrary property of a bit string that has been shown to correspond to the difficulty of guessing its bit identities. Entropy is never negative, and zero entropy corresponds to straightforward accurate guessing. Entropy increases with the size of the string, and decreases with the existence of order, or pattern among its bits. A bit string comprised of n bits is said to have zero pattern when persistent attempts to guess the bit identity of every bit based on knowledge of the identities of the other $(n-1)$ bits result in guessing right about $n/2$ of the bits. Such a string is regarded as "random." Then we conclude that to defeat fraudulent attempts to guess the money string, one should use a random string of sufficient bit size.

Theoretically speaking, a random string cannot carry any contents, any interpretive message (otherwise it will not be random), and hence the bit identities of a desired random string would not be able to carry its coin value. What else is there if not the identities of the comprising bits? Only one property is left (we recall that the string has no physicality, it is just some n bits, $\{0,1\}^n$ in order); the property is the bit size – the value of n.

A most secure digital coin will therefore be a random string comprised of some n bits, where the value of the coin, v_{coin} is some value of n, and n alone! $v_{\text{coin}} = v(n)$. The most obvious way to reduce the chance of deceitful guessing is to increase the size of the bit string.

The value function $v(n)$ may be computed on the basis of some arbitrary m parameters: $v_{\text{coin}} = v(n, a_1, a_2, \dots a_m)$ allowing for a rich variety of payment and coin splitting procedures. For example, let $v_{\text{coin}}(n) = a_0 + a_1 n$. This coin can be split to r coins: $v_1, v_2, \dots v_r$, where $v_i = (a_0/r)(n_i/(n/r)) + a_1 n_i$, n_i is the number of bits in coin v_i, and the split coins add up to the presplit coin: $v = v_1 + v_2 + \dots v_r$. Or, given $v_{\text{coin}} = v(n) = a_0 + a_1 n$, one could modify it to $v_{\text{coin}} = v(n) = a_0' + a_1' n$, where $a_0' = a_0 + a_1 n(1 - 1/q)$ and $a_1' = a_1/q$, and q is an arbitrary value. This easy-to-verify reframing allows one to change the coin resolution (e.g., number of bits per unit of currency).

The simplest form for the coin value function $v(n)$ will render it to be a rising monotonic function, namely that for $n_1 > n_2$, we will have $v(n_1) > v(n_2)$. This requirement will insure that the more valuable the coin, the greater its security – the smaller the chance for a successful guess of its value.

And we can reap another important benefit if we further restrict $v(n)$ to be "linear," namely to structure it such that $v(tn) = tv(n)$, where $0 < t < 1$. For a coin C with such a $v(n)$, one could split the coin string into two substrings: substring "A" comprising of bits 1 to k, where $k < n$, and substring "B" comprising of bits $(k + 1)$ to n. Whatever the value of k, the sum values of the substrings will always be the value of the original presplit coin: $v_{\text{coin}} = v_A + v_B$.

In practice, this will allow Alice who holds a coin C, valued, say $100, to split it to two smaller coins A and B, if she desires to pay Bob $32.75, and keep the change of $67.25 to herself. Bob will reapply the same procedure to further split his $32.75 to, say $12.50 that he wishes to pay Carla and the remaining $20.25 that he would keep for himself. This linear choice of $v(n)$ will allow Alice to split her coin to r coins, for any value of $r = 2, 3, ..,$ such that any holder of any split of such coin, would reapply the same procedure for further payments.

And if Alice wishes to make micropayment, the linear split will allow it. Suppose Alice signs up to a Wi-Fi service, or to movie library that charges $0.005/seconds. Alice, will line up a digital coin, worth, say $4.00, and pay for the service at 1-seconds intervals. If the value of n happens to be $n = 100,000$ bits, then Alice will simply split off 125 bits every second, and pass them to the server. Since the bit identities of Alice's coin are randomized, the chance for a thief to guess right each $0.005 is $2^{-125} = 1/4.25 \times 10^{37}$, quite negligible.

Nonrandomized Coins

Using a nonrandomized coin is also effective against brute-force guessing, despite the lower entropy of the coin. Such coins may express both their value and their identity through the identities of the comprising bits, offering a very rich range of possibilities to designate value, identity, terms of redemption, etc. The majority of digital coins are nonrandomized, or partly randomized. Such coins are subject to brute-force cryptanalysis, but offer effective expression of information. Unlike fully randomized coins, the nonrandomized coins don't betray their value through the count of their bits. Although it is noteworthy that randomized coins may obscure their value, and their count using a stream-masking mechanism. The idea being to embed randomized coins in a steady stream of randomized bits that have no value as coins.

Payment Activity Masking

"Naked" randomized coins may betray their value by their string size, and they, as well as nonrandomized coins may wish to hide payment activity between two specific nodes on the Internet. This can be done by activating a sufficiently strong flow of bits back and forth between the two nodes. These bits will be randomized and meaningless. When a node wishes to make a payment to the other, it encrypts the payment coin, and embeds it in the masking stream. The intended reader will be equipped with a cryptographic key to separate the wheat from the chaff, namely to spot the coin in the meaningless stream. The hacker will remain blind.

* * *

There are two broad philosophies as we mentioned before: self-anchored digital money, and claim check digital money. Both end up as a series of bits, and both can be tethered, and processed as discussed herein, but these two approaches are profoundly different. The most prominent self-anchored currency today is bitcoin, and it there where we turn next.

BITCOIN: THE VISION

Bitcoin exploded on the scene with a very definite and specific protocol for digital money (2008) leading to a faithful implementation of the protocol (2009) and a remarkable rise in popularity (2013). Soon enough imitators popped up, modifying this and that, vying for attention. Something called The Bitcoin Foundation was established, and its leaders are toying with the protocol. The bitcoin excitement attracted tens of thousands of our best developers and programmers striving to emerge with a better protocol, and to lead the pack. One would expect the original bitcoin to undergo major changes as it struggles for its position. Therefore, we will not dwell on the specifics of the original bitcoin in this account, but rather focus on the underlying principles that are shared by many of the baby bitcoins, emerging daily.

The main bitcoin principles are:

- Self-anchored
- Generating money by agreement to reward computational accomplishment
- Using transactional transparency to safeguard trading integrity
- Vulnerability to erosive cryptographic intractability
- Vulnerability to leadership corruption
- Finite amount of bitcoin

The most salient and remarkable attribute of bitcoin is its ability of being self-anchored. The second powerful idea is that it calls for money to be generated as a token of appreciation for having solved a mathematical challenge. The third principle is the block chain – the idea that every coin carries its ownership history with it, and that this history is also made public for the entire community to see. The fourth principle is the idea of masked traders – traders identified by a mask – code name that hides their true identity. The fifth principle is the idea that the bitcoin money scheme relies on modern erosive cryptography – ciphers that are assumed uncompromised today, but for which we have no guarantee as to how long they will remain secure, as they sustain a relentless cryptanalytic attack.

We will address these principles in turn, and discuss options for growth and modification.

Self-Anchored

Bitcoin is a network protocol that prescribes rules by which network nodes (traders) acquire and exchange units of a network-defined entity regarded as money, or "bitcoins." The bitcoin is defined with no regard to anything outside the network protocol. The bitcoin protocol could be exercised in total vacuum, in an empty universe, where there is nothing to be paid for by bitcoins. Bitcoins can be traded where the traders are unanimated computing devices. The bitcoin protocol neither identifies any reason for a trader to covet bitcoins nor any motivation for any player (trader) to pay bitcoins to another. In that respect, it is different from the traditional game of Monopoly, which also defines its own money, but it specifies Monopoly assets that can be bought with it. The bitcoin protocol is a "perpetuum mobile," it continues forever. Unlike Monopoly that is also a self-anchored money game, bitcoin has no winning point, no "end of game" state. Although the bitcoin protocol does not even prescribe a desired state by calling its self-created bitcoins "money," the bitcoin protocol tacitly assumes that traders would desire more of it.

Per definition, there is no need in the world outside bitcoin that can be satisfied with bitcoins. The outside world has no contact points, no overlapping with the bitcoin protocol, much as real-estate trade that has no contact, no overlap with Monopoly real-estate transactions.

On second thought, money, in its very essence ties together totally unrelated entities. There is no functional connection between, say, bananas, and a painting by Picasso. Albeit, money equates them, and spells out how many of the former are "worth" as much as the latter. Of course, the equation is anchored to the entity that makes it. For a monkey, even one banana is more valuable than all the paintings Picasso ever painted. And hence, bitcoin traders, who also live in "the real world," may equate and trade bitcoin against dollars, as well they do. People could equally well trade Monopoly dollars against US dollars, which, for some reason they don't do. Investors might grab a Picasso painting, which they have no appreciation for, reasoning that others do appreciate the artist and will be willing to pay for his painting – generating profit for the investor. And that is exactly how bitcoin is traded. Only that bitcoin is no work of art, no one appreciates it "as is" for its inherent attributes, it is coveted only because the current enthusiasm for it, is assumed to have staying power, inertia. Alas, the history of popularity of items with no inherent utility serves as an alarming thought. Hot articles of fashion drop out of sight; one-time collectors' items disappear; and yesterday's popular celebrities find themselves thoroughly ignored. There is no rational reason to suppose that the flare for bitcoins will last, and endure to render it into a currency that rivals the greenback, or the Pound Sterling.

As we discussed earlier, the US dollar is also self-anchored. Indeed, only that the US dollar mint has power and attributes not found in bitcoin.

The fact that there is no objective exchange value between bitcoin and any fiat currency, or between bitcoin and gold, for that matter, is alarming both for a total collapse of the bitcoin currency and for the persistent instability of its price.

Generating Money by Agreement to Reward Computational Accomplishment

For money to function, it can neither be too scarce nor too abundant. Central banks carefully control their fiat circulation. Earthly mined money is secured by hard work that provides a natural control: the higher the price, the more people are attracted to the effort to mine new quantities that eventually push the price down – and vice versa. But bitcoin denounces central banks, and must be fully defined in the context of a mathematical procedure – no physical digging and mining. So bitcoin replaced physical mining with mathematical mining.

What are the characteristics of physical mining? It is carried out on public land, it's rather a linear effort, and success is easy to prove. The term linear effort indicates that one has to go through a statistically defined amount of ore, in order to spot a small nugget of, say, gold. By sorting through double that amount, two nuggets of gold are likely to be spotted. And when gold is spotted, it is easy to show. The bitcoin designer copied these characteristics into his (her or its) elegant invention: the basis is a mathematical process known as hashing. Hashing is a process by which a long digital string, L, is reduced to a short digital string, S. It is very easy to hash L into S. But given S, it is believed difficult to unhash it to a long string L. Often times the fastest way to unhash S is to try one long string L, hash it quickly, and if it is not producing S, but another short string S', then to try again, with a different long string – hash it, check the hash, and continue further, until a long string is found such that it hashes to S. This search for a proper L is time intensive, and it is a linear effort, the best we can tell. So if the bitcoin community is challenged to race toward unhashing, then the community might honor the one who found the desired L first. Since hashing is one-way function, it is very easy for everyone to recognize that the unhashing challenge was solved – and therefore, the entire community will agree to grant the discoverer of that successful computation some bitcoin money.

Computation burden is very easy to gauge, and indeed the bitcoin protocol cleverly adjusts its mathematical mining in order to achieve the proper scarcity.

Using Transactional Transparency to Safeguard Trading Integrity

Double spending and fake money were the two fundamental challenges faced by digital money from its inception. Although the risk of fake money was met with some clever algorithmic tests, the risk of double spending had no resolution except for the requirement to invoke a central authority to validate the money in real time. Only such authority would possibly have the information needed to spot an attempt to reuse a digital coin. And lo and behold, the bitcoin designers devised a solution that is robust, and does not rely on a validating authority. And like most great ideas, the bitcoin solution is so utterly simple, that in retrospect one wonders how nobody thought about it earlier.

The bitcoin trading protocol calls for complete transactional transparency: every digital coin that changes hands will be registered as such on a public ledger, and on the coin itself. A payee then would readily verify that (1) what the coin the payer intends to pay is now owned by the payer, and (2) the payer has not paid with this coin before. Bitcoin very cleverly insures the integrity of that public ledger by cryptographic means that are none other than the computational tasks used to claim bitcoins through algorithmic mining.

This idea of public transparency of all transactions has never before come up for discussion, perhaps because digital money strives to emulate physical coins and paper bills that are passed hand to hand keeping both payer and payee anonymous to each other. Bitcoin managed to satisfy this anonymity requirement despite the transactional transparency. It did so with "masks": the traders wear masks, as a matter of speech, so the transparency, while complete, is maintained as far as the masks exist, not beyond. The identity of the trader who wears the mask remains hidden. It is the idea of masquerade balls where people carry out outrageous actions under the protection of a mask. Masking the traders is readily achieved via well-established cryptographic means. As a result, the transactions are in the open, but the traders themselves are cryptographically shielded.

This way bitcoin, very cleverly, creates anonymity and accountability, side by side.

It is noteworthy that the masks are not essential – in other words, one could exercise the bitcoin protocol with exposed traders' identity.

Vulnerability to Erosive Cryptographic Intractability

The entire cryptographic suite used by bitcoin is the erosive intractability kind, meaning: its usefulness is eroding with time, as computers become faster, and as mathematical insight becomes deeper. The rate of erosion depends on (1) the advancement in computer technology, and (2) the advancement in relevant mathematical insight. Both these factors advance in proportion to the pay-off of cryptanalysis of bitcoin. Say then that the more money that is denominated by bitcoin, the greater of a target it becomes, and the motivation to crack it is growing. It is virtually impossible to put an upper limit on how fast computers will become, and how much more knowledgeable in relevant math the hacker would get. Both factors are subject to human creativity and ingenuity where surprises are a matter of course.

The plain reality then is that bitcoin operates on borrowed time. No sooner will either one of its foundational cryptographic primitives succumb to its persistent cryptanalyst than bitcoin will melt down into zero capital. Although what is more likely is that a successful cryptanalyst would milk the system drop by drop to hide the fact that the crypto shield was cracked. She will exchange as many bitcoins as she can to dollars, euros, or some other fiat currency, and continue to do so until the cryptanalysis is discovered and bitcoin blows away.

Vulnerability to Leadership Corruption

Bitcoin has boxed itself into a very stringent demand, representing its motivational force: to keep the currency clean from abuse by some corrupt minority. The bitcoin movement sees the elite that runs the central banks as the root of all financial evil – as ill-suited custodians of the public trust. So they came up with money that is immunized against the potential abuse of a controlling minority. Instead of a secretive bank that keeps all the transactional data to itself, bitcoin offers the public ledger, exposing all transactions to the entire trading community. Similarly, its protocol draws its power by it being accepted by the traders. The robustness of bitcoin is argued by simulating attempts by a coordinated minority to preempt the currency, and proving mathematically how infeasible this is. Perhaps so, but for a system like bitcoin to be operational it does need the flexibility that is offered by a small management team with authority to intervene beyond an *a priori* rigid protocol. Where from does this team draw its authority? Bitcoin is silent about this. So traders organize through organs like The Bitcoin Foundation that takes upon itself all the necessary tweaking, adjusting, and specifying rules of the trade. Over time this management team will accumulate the power to control the destiny of the currency, and become the bitcoin version of the despised central banks. But because bitcoin operates on the high ground of allowing no minority to corrupt the currency, it finds itself being led *de facto* by a minority management team that is not subject to fair and well-stated mechanism of replacement, and upgrading. One might note that the much-derided central banks are an organ of democratically elected governments in any first-world democracy. Given the premises of human nature, it is just a matter of time before the bitcoin management team is infected by corruption.

Finite Amount of Bitcoins

The original bitcoin protocol imposes a ceiling as to the number of bitcoins in the "game." Accordingly the bitcoin trade is divided to two phases: (1) the phase when bitcoins are generated, and (2) the phase where the finite amount of allowed bitcoins is traded back and forth.

The motivation for this rigid limit is the inbred fear of runaway inflation, of the scenario where central banks go wild, and issue more and more of their fiat currency. On the other end, a finite amount of coins may result in shortage of coins. This can be helped by deflating the currency, and by trading with smaller and smaller fractions of one bitcoin.

Since the limit of bitcoin is arbitrarily imposed in the original protocol, it is highly likely that if the need arises, the prevailing bitcoin leadership will readjust the limit. Alternatively one could open up a bitcoin-2 traded with the same protocol, eventually matching its price with bitcoin-1, and allowing cross-trading. This will double the allowable coins, and it can be used iteratively to up the number at will.

BITCOIN STRUGGLE FOR IMPACT AND SURVIVAL

The Bitcoin saga is one where a tantalizing dream is puffed over a money protocol that cannot carry the day. It must be fundamentally modified. The bitcoin camp knows that, and struggles to change and adjust its premises at the margins without destroying its core. What is likely to happen is a split: a bitcoin faithful to the original protocol will tug along the financial parade in a marginal, risk-recognized fashion, and a bitcoin faithful to the grand idea of digital money will allow its present core to be modified and fit into the larger framework of digitized fiat currencies.

Let us review the necessary modifications to keep bitcoin impactful and surviving.

Stability

Being self-anchored, bitcoin is inherently unstable and it operates with the constant risk of total collapse. The way to handle this titanic difficulty is either to (1) hook the bitcoin to an external source of value, or (2) control the price with a large counter weight. The former will rob bitcoin of its original "soul," but the latter will have a chance to keep bitcoin going with its spirit intact, although some of its original principles bruised.

Hooking Bitcoin to an External Source of Value

To modify bitcoin so that its currency buys a certain commodity today, and does so tomorrow, it is necessary to reset the protocol. Let's analyze how a Bitcoin:Reset will look like:

The most troubling aspect of unreset bitcoin is its inherent instability. The fundamental solution to this problem, of course, is a replay of the way fiat currencies achieve their stability. Only in this case the price-stability agent (PSA) should be established as part of the Bitcoin:Reset protocol.

The PSA would be funded through the very noninnovative mechanism called taxation. Money would be collected as a percentage of a transaction (other taxation mechanisms are possible), and the tax-funded PSA would divide its holdings; with 50% going to bitcoins and 50% to a fiat currency, say US dollars. Over time, these holdings would increase and enable PSA to intervene in a counter-flow mode. When the bitcoin price soars, the PSA would flood the market with bitcoins. When the price loses ground, the PSA would buy them up. The effect would be proportional to the PSA's financial power.

But who should design the PSA protocol? Unreset bitcoin is run by a largely unchallenged, self-appointed cabal that tweaks the rules here and there. To be durable, serious, and transparent, the bitcoin steering committee will have to be elected by the community it manages. Workable – but how will the bitcoin election protocol be set up? For example, would it be proportional to bitcoin wealth? A good reset idea is needed to allow the PSA, elections, enhancements of algorithms, and so on, to take place.

Here is a reset idea: BitMint is a nonspeculative crypto currency that trades at par with the US dollar. It offers all the well-civilized and enticing goodies offered by bitcoin, and more. But, of course, it is centralized, so it does not pass the Satoshi Nakamoto test of not requiring trust in fallible human beings. If you pay or get paid with BitMint, you implicitly trust the BitMint mint.

Recently, the BitMint team developed a powerful protocol that enables a community of BitMint traders to shift at once to a decentralized trading regimen, and in such a way that the traders, or a subset thereof, can reverse the transition (if they are not happy with it), re-entering the centralized BitMint trading protocol.

Now, what does that mean? It means the bitcoin community is hereby invited to trade in a BitMint-centralized mode for a time, and use this time to unhurriedly develop a robust protocol covering all the points that need review and adjustment, taking on elections, the PSA, and so on. At a preset time, trading would emerge from the "centralized womb" into decentralized freedom, with all its engineering perfectly designed.

And fancy that: while newborn babies don't have the option to return to the womb for more "cooking," Bitcoin:Reset can be reversed to its centralized origins. Bitcoin:Reset will not only offer the means to "change shoes" for the long march toward success but also attract main-street attention. As the PSA proves itself, and as the current self-appointed back-room bitcoin executives are properly elected, the risk may deflate to acceptable levels and the average Joe may buy his beer with Bitcoin:Reset and even may opt to receive his paycheck in this currency.

By way of analogy, consider the US Declaration of Independence. Written in the stress and rush of the emergence of this epic story we call the United States of America, this document eventually led to that much longer, much more deliberate effort by many of the same visionaries – the US Constitution.

Unreset bitcoin was catapulted into the limelight before its design had a chance to mature and be refined, so let's reset the currency and re-establish it on deliberate, well-thought premises.

Internal Bitcoin Stabilizer

Here is a fantasy: a trader called Santa Claus is in possession of unlimited funds, and is committed to keep bitcoin trading stable. Santa will set up a target price for a bitcoin, denominated in some fiat currency, say, US dollars. If the present price of a bitcoin is below the target price, then Santa will buy a lot of bitcoins until it reaches the target price. And if the price of a bitcoin is higher than the target value, then Mr. Claus will dump bitcoins on the market. As long as Santa has funds to apply, he can nail the price to its desired target value, regardless of the fact that bitcoin is self-anchored.

The problem with this fantasy is that it calls for an altruistic trader. Alas, last count, not many of them showed up. The alternative is to modify the bitcoin protocol to construct such a "Santa Claus" trader: built by the community, and serving the community. This will take the form of the PSA, described in the immediately preceding section: the traders will agree to pay a small portion from each trade to build the fortunes of the stabilizer (Santa Claus), to help the community to keep the price stable.

This construction (of the PSA) will be effective in extinguishing small-scale fluctuations of price, but since its funds are limited, the PSA will eventually succumb to a price movement that it cannot contain. One might argue that if bitcoin is doomed to succumb to a total price collapse, it is better for this to happen early when the total wealth expressed in bitcoins is smaller, the number of victims smaller, the measure of destruction smaller.

Bitcoin Vulnerability to Erosive Cryptographic Intractability

This vulnerability is least likely to be addressed. For the vast majority of traders the crypto is fine. It is based on primitives that have been around for years – ostensibly uncracked, and as such they are expected to remain intact for the foreseeable future – so believes the average bitcoin trader. And since any in-depth discussion of the erosive intractability of bitcoin is fast deteriorating into obscure mathematics, it is simply ignored and assumed a nonissue.

As a result, the most likely scenario for bitcoin is that in proportion to its popularity its crypto shield will be attacked, and during bitcoin lifetime its shield will be cracked. The crackers will exploit their feat very smartly, stealing bitcoins in relatively small amounts. The victims will hardly have a credible complaint because of the anonymity of the trade. The rightful owner will not be able to prove his ownership claim if the counter claim comes from someone who has the same private key.

Alternatively, the bitcoin community will keep improving the underlying crypto primitives, and some cabal of leadership will decide when to replace the old primitives. A durable solution will be to replace the class of erosive intractability primitives with a class of equivocation-based primitives, which would solve this vulnerability. See more in the appendix.

Bitcoin Vulnerability to Leadership Corruption

It will become increasingly clear that bitcoin requires leadership with the authority to make changes as fast as circumstances require. The need to have this leadership elected by the community will also become very clear. So some mechanism would be agreed upon to let the body of bitcoin traders transfer power to one or few leaders who will take the responsibility to make the necessary decisions. All the changes discussed herein have to be decided upon by a leadership that is legitimized by periodic elections, and so most immunized against the human curse of corruption.

Attacks on Bitcoin

Bitcoin, young and exciting, flawed but hopeful, already faces a slew of adversaries and enemies. First, the governments that stand to lose their control over the money used by their citizens will use all their power to keep bitcoin as a sideshow. Second, the ever-growing number of bitcoin imitators will attack and shave off this currency to build their own. But the killer force for bitcoin in its original form is expected to be the fiat-money extended currencies: the digital money that respects and digitizes the prevailing fiat currencies, extending them to digital format where it competes with bitcoin offering similar conveniences, and advantages.

DIGITIZED FIAT MONEY AND OTHER COMMODITIES

Every form of money ever paid with some success has been an extension of the form of money used before. This is no accident, and not even limited to money: every concept in math, every idea in science, every creative art are built over the previous reality that they come to enhance, or replace. Human mental and spiritual histories emulate our biological evolution – *we evolve*. The original adaptation of rare metals as money, was a way to create a universal medium to replace local money in the form of items precious for local communities. The idea of minted coins removed the inconvenience of dragging a scale every-where; paper money is light, at any denomination, stores well, and prints well. And today we extend this paper money to become a digital string regardless of the media it is written on. Bitcoin goes a step further, calls for money in a digital form that is arising from an algorithm that claims no ancestry in any former form of money. This violation of the evolution principle may prove the fatal flaw of this clever and exciting currency. All the other attributes of bitcoin can be secured with digital currencies that simply extend fiat currency, or, say extend any commodity.

First, we shall describe Fiat-Bitcoin: a currency that mimics bitcoin in every way except that a fiat-bitcoin has a fixed exchange value against a choice of fiat currency. We will then describe digital currencies that have no overlap with bitcoin. It's important to note that the powerful notion of tethered money applies to them all.

Fiat.Bitcoin Currency

Fiat.Bitcoin is a digital currency protocol based on nonspeculative digital currency that is traded via a bitcoin anonymity and double-spending control protocol, mandating that the anonymous traders will register with the mint via their public key, and as condition for trading, will agree to reveal their true identity against a properly executed court order. The key differences between Fiat.Bitcoin and the original (2008) bitcoin are:

- Trade is carried out by passing digital strings that reflect a well-defined measure of a desired commodity, like fiat currencies, gold, silver, real estate, etc. The value of the string is nonspeculative, it redeems for the same amount that it was purchased for.
- Trading is specified, managed, controlled, and is under the responsibility of the digital mint that announces it, and establishes it.
- The anonymity of traders is safeguarded and respected unless a specific court order breaches it.

The key similarity between nominal (2008) bitcoin and Fiat.Bitcoin is: The protocol for anonymity and prevention of double spending is essentially the same.

Protocol: A Fiat.Bitcoin mint issues digital strings as claim checks against US dollars. It offers its traders to use their credit card, or banking account to send US dollars to the Fiat.Bitcoin mint, against which they receive a bit string that is always redeemable against the same amount of US dollars used to purchase it. The trader also passes on a personal public key to the mint. The bit string issued by the mint to the trader is cryptographically signed by the mint (using its private key) to allow every examiner to verify its validity (via the mint's public key). The signed coin will designate the public key of the purchaser as the current owner of the coin. The owner can then "play" in the bitcoin environment set forth by the mint. That is, he or she can pay the coin, or part thereto to another trader in the same bitcoin-like trading environment. The payer will effect the transaction using his or her private key, and the recipient's (the payee's) public key. The transaction will be submitted for approval, and together with other transactions in the same time frame, will form a "block" that would be examined for absence of fraud and will be signed for validation. The signature of the block will be carried out either by the mint that runs the "show" or by fellow traders, who are motivated by a specified fee paid by the payer and the payee in prespecified proportions (all the specifications are the responsibility of the mint). This is similar to the published 2008 bitcoin protocol, once all the possible bitcoins have been mined. The mint will change the fee for the signer to insure proper balance between computational burden and speed of transactions. The new owner of the described coin will be able to reapply this bitcoin protocol to transact the coin, or part thereto to a third trader, and on it goes. Traders may own a number of pairs of public–private keys, and "fake" transactions between them. Any current owner of a Fiat.Bitcoin coin may, at his or her discretion, hand this coin over to the Fiat.Bitcoin mint, asking for redemption. The mint will verify the history of ownership of the coin, or part thereto, as the case may be, and will redeem it to the claimant if all checks out.

In other words, Fiat.Bitcoin is exploiting the ingenious bitcoin trading protocol, but does so over nonspeculative money. The trading protocol constructs layers of security by having the next owner of a coin sign (lock) the full history of the coin. As a result, each turn of the coin adds another layer of security – more obstacles for any hacker.

Suppose that Alice purchased a $100 coin from that mint, then paid $80 from it to Bob per his "mask" (his public key), and then Bob paid the money or part thereto to Carla, and she did the same vs. David. This goes on and on, until Zelda decides to redeem the coin (or the part of it, she gets ownership of). The Fiat.Bitcoin mint will know, at most the identity of Alice and Zelda (the purchaser and the redeemer) of its coins, but will be clueless as to the identities of Bob, Carla, David, etc. through which the coin, or part thereto have passed. These "middle owners" will be protected by the cryptographic intractability of their public–private keys.

This state of affairs is perfectly analogous to Alice withdrawing $100 in cash from her bank account, paying it all, or sum of it to Bob, who pays from it to Carla, who pays to David, on an on, until Zelda gets a hold of some of that cash, and deposits it in her bank account. The bank may know who Alice and who Zelda are, but is clueless as to the identity of those in between.

Non-double spending, and privacy protection are preserved, as with the original bitcoin. However, should the authorities focus on a shady trade and spot a suspicious public key passing dirty money, then they would secure a court order and present it to the mint. The mint will contact the unknown public-key holder, and notify him or her that their money will not be redeemable upon demand, and their public key will be listed as noncompliant, and hence non-transactable, until such time that the public key owner comes forth and identifies himself or herself.

This is how the community of traders maintains its privacy, while allowing the law enforcement authorities to flash out bad actors. This scheme mimics the US Constitution Fourth Amendment which not only guarantees citizens their privacy against random and wonton police search but also allows the authorities to seek a court order for a privacy-invading search. As much as citizens value their privacy, they, by and large, would agree that these privacy rights should not be allowed to be abused by criminals or terrorists.

The exact measure of traders' privacy will be determined by the prevailing law in any trading community. It may range from zero privacy to total privacy. In some in-between cases, the Fiat.Bitcoin protocol may allow the purchasing trader, and the redeeming trader to identify themselves only through their public keys, and so even they will remain anonymous.

The Fiat.Bitcoin traders can readily split a coin to pay any amount thereof to any other trader.

This "hybrid" protocol may allow a trader to pay a coin to two or more traders on the basis of signing off by "each," "all," or "some," requirements regarding paying that coin further. For instance, a high-ranking supervisor will sign off on some specified payment, if her underlying accountant did so earlier.

Special Purpose Fiat.Bitcoins: Digital mints may set up bitcoin-trading environments subject to a variety of terms. In some, the traders will have to qualify according to some preset qualifiers. In others, the traders will participate in financial investment and prospecting. In yet others, the traders will enjoy a steady stream of interest income while they trade in the Fiat.Bitcoin environment. One must note that any commodity may become the basis of a Fiat.Bitcoin environment.

Stock.Fiat.Bitcoin: A particular nonspeculative mint may be set forth where the digital coins will be issued against a particular stock or a particular financial instrument of any kind. The mint will deposit the stock, as it does with cash, ready at any moment to redeem the same. The Fiat.Bitcoin traders will trade the same as aforementioned. Any trader will be able to ask the mint to redeem any bitcoin she owns, and against which she will receive the nominal amount of deposited stock. The "betting" element here is with respect to the dollar value of the redeemed stock. If the Fiat.Bitcoin-traded stock will rise in value, traders might expect it to continue to appreciate, and go on trading with it. If it loses value, the traders might all rush to redeem their stock assets. The point here is that traders will be able to readily use the stock as money, and gamble on its future worth. Such Fiat.Bitcoin stocks will be regarded as stock.Fiat.Bitcoin

Interest.Fiat.Bitcoin: Since the deposits that traders make with the mint may be deposited in an interest-bearing bank account, the mint could offer to split this interest with the traders. This will allow traders to "play" and "trade" with each other in that bitcoin-trading environment while their money accumulates interest, as if it were deposited and not used. In addition, it might have a durability impact on the coin, or otherwise impact the behavior of the traders. The mint will manage its profits by adjusting the fee it charges for purchasing an interest-bearing digital coin, as well as its redemption fee. The higher the prevailing interest, the more attractive this coin.

Analysis: Fiat.Bitcoin identifies the anonymity and double-spending prevention protocol as the "nugget" of the bitcoin innovation, and applies it over non-speculative, fiat-money digital currencies, in an environment where a multitude of interconnecting mints is forming a global network – the InterMint, and is set forth to evolve into the rise of a superstable global currency.

Fiat.Bitcoin will be applicable to virtually all the bitcoin imitators popping up daily. The diversification of the bitcoin concept into a multitude of distinct algorithms, each compliant with the shared abstract solution, is a considerable remedy to the risk of compromising the single algorithm on which the original (2008) bitcoin relies.

Fiat.Bitcoin is based on the notion of a managing mint that builds a bitcoin-trading environment under its rules and responsibility. It solves the inherent bitcoin problem of the rigidity of the majority – a rigidity that prevents any executive minority from taking timely steps to safeguard the trading dynamics from eventual spiraling collapse. The mint is also the address for complaints, conflict resolution, and any challenges for wrongdoing. On the other hand, the concept of the InterMint based on ever-growing interconnecting mints, presents the trading public with a broad spectrum and choice for mints to trust. Eventually well-managed, fair, supportive mints will become more popular – not by decree, not by choicelessness – but by public demand.

The managing mint will also be a convenient address for law enforcement to present a court order to expose the identity of a trader under suspicion.

The variety of commodity-based, nonspeculative mints will be cascaded to "cocktail" mints through several rounds that end up establishing one or few global currencies which rely on a broad spectrum of desirable and shared commodities – the wealth of society. This reliance endows these superdigital currencies with a durable stability. Stable global currency is the necessary framework for a smooth and effective global trade, and it serves as the necessary condition for a bold credit market. It is credit that serves as the leverage for human prosperity.

In summary, Fiat.Bitcoin takes up the shinny nugget in bitcoin, shakes off the overreaching quest to generate money without a foundation of human utility, and corrects for its risk of relying on a single unproven algorithm, by creating the InterMint which relies on a multitude of specific implementation of the brilliant bitcoin concept of anonymity trading, and double-spending prevention.

Fiat Digital Currency: Claim Check Format

Alice deposits $100 with Bob, against which Bob returns a claim check that says: the bearer of this claim check is owed $100 payable by Bob. Bob then encodes this message in a digital string. That digital string constitutes digital currency in a claim-check format. No elaborate trading protocol is required – though allowed; no block chains are mandatory – though optional, and of course no speculation as to how many dollars this digital string will fetch. It is $100 today, tomorrow, rain or shine.

The original motivation to digitize dollars (or euros, yuan, gold... etc.) was network anonymity. Payment in cyber space was based on mutual identification of payer and payee. That means that anyone with a watchful eye could spy on any cyber-space trader as to what he or she buys and sells online. Come to think about it, the record of what we buy over time is a pretty powerful "X-ray machine" into the very persona that we are, into our mood, and disposition; what clothes we buy, what shoes, what restaurants we frequent, where we fly, what we do for pleasure, to whom we send flowers, etc. He who uses cyber space as his town square submits to life in a fish bowl. The pioneers of digital currency were moved by this sense of discomfort, vying to construct a payment protocol that would allow the payer to remain anonymous, as cash payers are in a brick-and-mortar store. It was clear from the beginning that such anonymity will also serve the dark side for those who have criminal acts to hide, but for many the model for striking the proper balance was the fourth amendment to the US Constitution that keeps police outside any private property, unless the police persuades a competent judge that there exists "probable cause" for a criminal activity that justifies a search warrant. It is clear the criminals exploit this protection, but for the majority of Americans it's a fair balance, much like the speeding limit – if cars are forced to move slower, there will be less fatal accidents, but the price of wholesale inconvenience is deemed excessive. These "blue sky" thoughts regarding digital currency were so guided.

Most readers will be surprised to hear that in the early 1990s, the notion of digital currency rose to become an active research issue within the cryptographic community. The most prominent researcher and developer was David Chaum, who eventually challenged the market with his pioneering company DigiCash. Chaum's solutions ideas are brilliant and robust, his answer to the anonymity issue is clean and effective, and relies on still-powerful cryptographic primitives. But he showed up too early and had to fold, unable to make his case. (Nothing is so pathetic as an idea whose time has not yet come.) Yet, evolutionary steps took place away from the public limelight. They are making an appearance today, positioned to capture the public excitement with bitcoin. As bitcoin flaws hold it back from storming the financial landscape, the most robust versions of claim-check centralized digital currency are coming forth.

In the pages ahead, we will discuss the Chaum's solution representing the original digital money ideas, and the modern ideas for nonspeculative, claim-check type, money in a digital format.

Early Claim-Check Digital Money

The original concern that led to early digital money was buyer's privacy. A suitor buying a bouquet of flowers to his paramour may wish to protect his identity. A timid fellow buying a *Guide to Stop Blushing in Public* would wish to pay with cash. Ordinary folks uneasy about their exposure to the credit card companies also would welcome an easy yet anonymous payment method. This concern was resolved with the invention of the public–private key contraption.

It worked as follows: Alice paid the bank $100, and received in return a digital statement saying: "The bearer of this statement may claim $100 from the bank. This claim check has a serial number, say: 1234. Alice then goes shopping in a faraway pharmacy where she buys some medications and medical devices that suggest that she might suffer from some embarrassing ailment, so she wishes to remain anonymous. She therefore keeps her credit card in her wallet, and uses, instead, the $100 claim check. The pharmacist does not accept this open statement because as far as she is concerned, Alice fabricated the claim check, and the bank would not honor it.

To alley the pharmacist fears, Alice asks the bank to sign the digital statement with the bank's secret private key. (She does so when she purchases the digital money.) The signature, which is some form of encryption, S, of the claim check, C, is now forwarded along with C for the pharmacist examination. Alice then tells the pharmacist: The "gibberish" looking data string, S, is encryption of the bank's claim check, C. The encryption was carried out using the bank's private key. Only the bank has this key, so the existence of the signature S is a proof that the claim check C was signed by the bank, and was not fabricated by Alice.

"How do I know that S is the encryption of C using the bank's secret key?" asks the pharmacist.

"Simple," answers Alice, "the bank has published on its website its public key – the key that corresponds to the bank's secret key. Now you use the published public key, and decrypt the signature S with it. The pharmacist does so and indeed the signature S turns into the claim check C. This could only have happened if S were encrypted (signed) using the bank's private key. In other words, the pharmacist carried out a test that proves to her that Alice has not written a dummy claim check. The claim check was encrypted, and hence issued by the bank. Once the pharmacist is satisfied, he releases the merchandise to Alice, and forwards the claim check to the bank for redemption. The bank performs the same test, then verifies that this claim check was not redeemed before and credits the pharmacist for $100.

Alice achieves her goal of remaining anonymous toward the pharmacist. Her identity was not compromised. Alas, the service bank has a record that claim check number 1234 was issued to Alice. Ordinarily the bank will not know what exactly Alice purchased with the claim check, but if a need arises, a very short conversation with the pharmacist might violate Alice's privacy (unless that state has some strong privacy laws).

David Chaum found an elegant way to keep the identity of Alice private before the merchant on one hand, and before the bank on the other hand. Chaum's protocol preserves Alice's privacy even against a collaborative attempt by the bank and the merchant to join forces and breach Alice's identity.

David Chaum's Anonymity

Chaum's idea is based on simple and sound procedure that persuades the bank to *blindly* sign (encrypt) a statement that Alice claims obligates the bank to pay $100 to its bearer. Why in the world would a bank agree to blindly sign such a statement, and allow itself to be a victim of a fraud? After all, the blind statement could have said that the bank owes $1,000,000 to the bearer!

Upon first hearing about it, most, if not all, will say: Not in a thousand years! No bank will ever agree to own a debt without reading how big that debt is. And yet, banks willingly and blindly sign such a statement once they understand Chaum's idea.

David Chaum achieved the blind signature by employing a cryptographic primitive that does not rely on erosive intractability, which is the common modality of modern cryptography; instead, Chaum based his solution on durable probability. The rest of Chaum's solution though, does rely on erosive intractability.

Alice prepares, say, 1000 statements C_1, C_2, ...C_{1000} that each say: "The bank hereby obligates itself to pay the bearer of this statement, the sum of $100." Each statement is marked by a randomly selected serial number. Alice then uses her secret cipher and encrypts each of the 1000 statements into signatures (cryptograms) S_1, S_2,....S_{1000} and submits the 1000 encrypted statements to the bank.

The bank will receive from Alice her decryption key, and randomly pick 999 secret statements for decryption. Lo and behold, all these 999 secret statements decrypt to the aforementioned statement, namely they commit the bank to $100, each.

So observing, the bank will be prepared to sign the last statement in the set *without* decrypting it. The reason: The chance for fraud is 1/1000, or 0.1% because Alice had no clue which of her statements will be the one not decrypted. The chance for the nondecrypted one to be the signed one is exactly 1/1000. If any of the decrypted 999 signatures comes through as a fraud, say, obligating the bank for $1000, then the bank would have cancelled the deal, mark Alice as a fraudster, and would never do any more business with her. Alice should be very uneducated with probabilities to venture such a fraud. When the blindly signed statement comes back to the bank to be honored, the bank can't tie this statement to Alice, it could have been prepared by any other trader. Obviously, the more traders in this protocol, the greater the privacy of each trader.

In the worst case, by exercising this procedure with many traders, the bank would lose 0.1%, which for the $100 statements amounts to losing 10 cents per case. If the bank sets its service fee to be a quarter per deal, then the bank's profit per deal will be between 25 cents (best case) and 15 cents (worst case). Banks are not alien to probability calculus, they use it to appraise credit risk, determine the amount of reserve in their coffers, and offer different interest rates for different deposit time spans.

The choice of 1000 statements is pedagogical; it obviously could be a much larger number (making fraud even less likely). All the encryption and decryption is carried out automatically and instantaneously.

Chaum also used a clever crypto primitive that allows Alice to reverse the bank's blind signature to the same signature that would have been produced by the bank, had it seen the preencrypted statement written by Alice. Chaum's brilliance is in the fact that Alice can reverse the blind signature issued by the bank (over Alice's encrypted statement) to the signature of the unencrypted statement, without knowing the bank's encryption key. All in all, Alice submits to the merchant the signature of her plaintext statement. The merchant behaves exactly as before, decrypting the signature submitted by Alice, using the bank's public key, and so being satisfied of the validity of the bank's stated obligation.

At the end of the day, even if the merchant and the bank get together, they cannot pierce Alice's anonymity. The bank collects the service fee, the merchant gets to sell his merchandise (rather than losing it to the next vendor, who participates in the solution), and Alice retains her privacy with respect to her purchase. This also means that the government is in the dark as to who bought this merchandise, no pressure on the bank or the merchant will yield this information.

Modern Claim-Check Digital Money

David Chaum's digital-money design shares with bitcoin the vulnerability to erosive intractability threatening to collapse the entire money system. Should an adversary figure out how to deduce the bank's secret key from the published public key, it would be straightforward for that adversary to construct fake signed statements that would be duly verified by the merchant, and eventually honored by the bank. Remember, in Chaum's scheme the bank does not see what it signs, so the bank has no means to spot the fraudulent statement of obligation as opposed to the bona fide one. The breach of the cryptography would be clear when the bank is broke.

Modern digital-money solutions make a distinction between the risk to the bank and the risk to the traders.

Digital Money Primary Risk

The first and foremost objective of a digital-money system is to insure that the money itself, and the mint that issues it, will not be fatally compromised. A money system should be designed for infinite duration, and hence even a very small chance for a fatal attack on the money itself is intolerable. This realization, arguably, disqualifies any digital money system that is based on erosive intractability, where the rate of erosion is unpredictable.

The other catastrophic scenario for digital currency is the "run-on-the-bank": a situation where many, even all the traders converge on the mint to redeem their digital claim checks. If the mint behaves like a deposit bank, then it falters on that occasion. To avoid this paralytic scenario, the mint must store the deposits in a ready-to-be-claimed fashion.

The first risk, counterfeit, is handled with the old-fashioned way: book-keeping. Minted digital coins are logged as redeemable, and once redeemed are logged as such. The mint will not redeem a coin it did not mint, nor will it redeem the same coin twice. By sticking to this simple procedure, the mint will not sustain a catastrophic loss of its capital. It may redeem a coin to its thief, but that does not bankrupt the mint. Clearly, the books of the mint are the heart of the operation. If they become compromised, the monetary system collapses. The counter statement, though, captures the strength of the digital mint: the money system will not collapse as long as the integrity of the coin database in the mint stays intact. The most important security feature here is that the battle-grounds have shrunk around the mint, where security can concentrate, rather than let money be stored while vulnerable in thousands of financial institutions, each of which may spurn a leak. Since the coin data *per se* needs only to be written once, it can be readily etched onto inerasable media, or at least into nonrewritable media. Any number of copies can be made of the mint, and if the coin data is written through highly randomized bits then layers of security can be structured, as we discussed in Chapter 3, and so secure the mint further.

The InterMint – a networked set of mints will be another security means. If the money in circulation is minted by n mints then compromising one mint will invalidate only $1/n$ of the circulated funds.

The primary risk will also extend to the deposits. If the digital money digitizes hard commodities like gold or silver, the mint faces the challenge to store the deposits with sufficient security and safety to be able to handle a violent attack from nature or man. Although every vault is associated with a nonnegligible break-in attack, and not even Ft. Knox comes with an absolute guarantee against a massive robbery, the position of digital currency is not worse than the currency represented by the digital commodity. So indeed a vault, or vaults keeping gold deposits secure to be redemption ready for any demand on the part of the digital-claim-check holders (the traders), will be as vulnerable to the digital representation money as it is to the commodity trading itself. No appreciable added risk on account of digitization.

Alas, if the digitized commodity is a modern fiat currency (e.g., dollar, yuan, euro) then a hyper situation arises: the deposits are digital entities too, and according to our security analysis in Chapter 3, they are less secure than the minted money. So while the mint relies on its high security, the deposits that back up the mint, and which are deposited in some normally secure bank, are themselves subject to hacking which is easier to do than to hack the digitally minted funds. The monetary system will collapse all the same if the deposits are compromised. This risk can be handled in ways symmetrical to the defense of the mint, namely, on one hand, the deposits could be spread among several banks, so that if one bank gets compromised the rest are still in good order, and on the other hand the larger the sum of the deposit, the more warranted this account is for layers and layers of security and protection. Nothing is guaranteed, but the table is set to favor the security efforts over the hacker's ambitions.

Digital Money Secondary Risk

The most serious aspect of the secondary risk is the fraudulent manufacture of copies of bona fide digital coins. If a hacker builds a fake coin, it will not wash with the mint, but if he manages to guess, steal, cheat himself into constructing a valid coin of untethered money, then the hacker would redeem it, since the mint will not be the wiser. Eventually the owner victim will try to redeem the same coin, and will be rejected. Although the mint does not lose money *per se*, if such bad losses proliferate, traders will exit from this digital currency, and the currency will collapse. The mint will not lose money, but will lose its enterprise.

The simplest attempt at fraud is brute-force guessing of a coin's digital make-up. A fraudster could try as many guesses as he chooses because the mint would not stop these redemption attempts lest they are issued by the rightful owner of the digital coin. Randomization of the coin content, and insuring sufficient size is the classic countermeasure against brute-force guessing. It is possible to extend the randomization to the full expression of the coin, as analyzed in Chapter 3.

Randomization offers another fundamental advantage: It voids the fraudulent favorite means – brute-force cryptanalysis. If the coin is *a priori* randomized, and then Alice encrypts it with cipher X when she passes the coin to Bob, then even if the hacker is aware of the cipher Alice used (X), he would not be able to use brute-force cryptanalysis because he would not have the feedback to guide him whether he hit the right key or not, since all the decrypted plaintexts are ostensibly randomized.

A hacker could attempt to cheat a trader either with a fake coin, or with a double-spent coin. The way to handle these risks is to combine the trade with a security certificate presented by the payer, and use his certified identity to prosecute a fraudster and ban him from further fraud – as one security method, along with real-time coin verification which can be engineered as we have seen in Chapter 3 via a network of authorization centers, some very close and local to dissolve any backlog and untoward waiting time.

Storage of digital money, or transfer between two parties with a secure shared key is carried out using any of the prevailing ciphers, all enjoy the freedom from brute-force attack when the coin bits are sufficiently randomized.

Transferring money between two strangers, or using "masked identities" will normally call for any of the prevailing public–private key pair ciphers. Most of these *privacy-between-strangers* actions rely on standard one-way functions that suffer from erosive intractability. They will not be protected by the randomization of the coins. New generation of probability-based tools will increase the security of trader-to-trader payment over insecure mode.

Anatomy of Ad-Hoc Payment

Alice and Bob are two strangers who meet in cyberspace. Alice is interested in something Bob has, and wishes to buy it from him. The price is $12.00. Bob has set up a website with e-commerce capabilities, and Alice fills in her payment data, and clicks "pay." Bob now has everything he needs to defraud Alice by posting another charge for any nonoutrageous amount, trusting that Alice will overlook it in her monthly statement when she reviews it one late night, half asleep, some 3 weeks later. His chances to defraud her are excellent!

What happened here? Alice surrendered to a stranger, Bob, the vital financial data that allows him to defraud her for as long as the payment card she used is valid. Fraudsters used to charge one outrageous sum from card data, which was quickly discovered, and the card voided. Now they push through small charges on a recurrent basis, and statistically, most victims don't even realize they are defrauded. The public statistics published by a new startup, BillGuard, explains it. BillGuard spots these frauds through a sophisticated inference engine built by former cyber spies in the Israeli defense forces. They flash out hundreds of dollars of annual fraud on average, unsuspecting citizens. (Fair disclosure: BillGuard founder and CEO, Yaron Samid, is the son of the author).

In the coming digital currency world, Alice would buy a couple of hundreds of dollars to charge her phone with, and click the $12.00 purchase directly to Bob. Bob will validate the money bit string with the respective mint, and send Alice the merchandise. If the merchandise is digital, Bob might have zero information about Alice (she might even use a fake name, or give no name at all). If the merchandise needs shipping, then Bob will know Alice's shipping address that might also be a holding company from where Alice claims the merchandise with a password. Bob surely has no data to effect any fraudulent charges against Alice.

The digital money transfer from Alice to Bob is carried out via a secure session protocol (Ad-Hoc Cyber Security), similar to the transfer of payment data, but unlike the payment card protocol, it is not vulnerable to the man-in-the-middle (MiM) fraud.

Ad-Hoc Cyber Security

Alice and Bob, two strangers on cyber space have no opportunity for *a priori* private conversation. They cannot use regular encryption because they never met before, and had no chance to exchange a secure encryption key. If they exchange the key on cyber space then Eve the eavesdropper, and Harry the hacker will spot it and use it to compromise Alice's and Bob's bilateral privacy. For a while this situation was considered helpless, albeit during the 1970s several ingenious cryptographic tools were invented and enabled Alice and Bob to forge a private channel while being listened to by their adversaries. The first to crack this conceptual wall was Ralph Merkle who has invented a method for Alice and Bob to share a secret on a temporary basis. His idea was simple: Alice will prepare a set of computational problems (say, a 1000 problems), that would require, say, 2 min to solve (each). The solution produces two numbers: x and y. Alice solves all the problems, and tabulates the result. (The numbers of 1000 problems, and 2 min are for pedagogical reasons only). Alice then makes these 1000 problems public, and instructs Bob to randomly choose one of these problems and solve it. When done, Bob is instructed to communicate to Alice his result for the x variable – and nothing more. Bob, randomly picks, say, problem #712, and computes $x_{712} = 4,567,893$, and $y_{712} = 98,257,112$. He communicates x_{712} to Alice, but keeps y_{712} to himself. Alice checks her table, and finds that $x = 4,567,893$ corresponds to problem #712. She then tells Bob, let's use the number you computed for y_{712} as our private secret, which Eve the eavesdropper and Harry the Hacker are blind about.

Indeed, y_{712} is unknown to Eve and Harry because they don't have the solution table that Alice has. They will have to solve Alice's problems one by one. On average they will have to solve 500 problems before they encounter $x_{712} = 4,567,893$, and then discover the secret code: $y_1 = 98,257,112$. This will last on average $2 \times 500 = 1000$ min, or 16 + hours in which Alice and Bob will use a secret code to conduct and conclude their private business. The genius in Merkle's idea is the random choice of the problem (illustrated by the choice of problem #712). Random choice cannot be anticipated, credibly predicted, or expected by however supersmart an algorithm may be. Alas, Ralph Merkle's solution idea is cumbersome and somewhat tedious, nonetheless, it is robust and effective.

Diffie and Hellmann joined with Ralph Merkle to improve on his concept. The former eventually came up with the brilliant Diffie and Hellman concept: They found a mathematical environment that enabled Alice and Bob to each compute the same number from different input. It's like computing $30 = 2 \times 15$ and $30 = 5 \times 6$. Given a set of natural numbers S both Alice and Bob choose a random number in S, referring to it as a private key. Each then computes a corresponding number in S, which is regarded as the corresponding public key. Alice and Bob make their public keys public. A given formula takes in Alice's private key and Bob's public key to compute a shared key K while the same formula is used by Bob to compute the shared key from his private key and Alice's public key. Eve and Harry only know the public keys, not the private keys, so they can't compute the shared key. Diffie–Hellman works smoothly for almost all the e-commerce transactions in the world.

Since each public key is computed from its corresponding private key, it stands to reason that the public key will reverse compute to the private key. And it does, only that we hope it is hard enough to do, to prevent this computation from finishing up in time to harm us.

Soon afterward, a trio of cryptographers: Rivest, Shamir, and Adelman (better known through the acronym RSA) has revisited the foundation of cryptography and concluded that one of its fundamental premises can be challenged. Throughout the history of cryptography the encryption key was the same, or very similar to the decryption key. The RSA pioneers realized that the decryption key should reverse the action of the encryption key, but it should not necessarily be the same. And indeed they carved out a mathematical niche where an encryption key E_k and a decryption key D_k were different from each other; nonetheless a plaintext encrypted with E_k was reversed by applying D_k. Alice could now give Bob her encryption key that he would use to encrypt his private communication to her, and since she never gave out the corresponding decryption key, she would be the only one able to reverse Bob's ciphertext to his plaintext. Bob did the same vis-a-vis Alice: He sent her his encryption key that produced a ciphertext that only he could interpret.

Ralph Merkle, Diffie–Hellmann, and RSA provide means for Alice and Bob to establish a private channel in the wilderness of cyberspace, despite being strangers and deprived of an *a priori* secure channel to exchange a secret encryption key.

By now we have more mathematical solutions that work in the same way that Merkle, Diffie–Hellmann, and RSA work, and many more uses were invented for them. As we enjoy and celebrate this feat that underlies e-commerce, we should keep in mind that Diffie–Hellman and RSA (as well as their newer similar solutions) are all under the spell of erosive intractability. Given the public key in each case, it is clearly possible to derive and compute the corresponding private key. Once the private key is compromised, the viability of the compromised trading system is crashing. We hope that our adversary finds it hard to timely deduce the private key from the public key, but we have no proof to substantiate this hope. We do know for sure that whatever the initial intractability of these algorithms, over time this intractability succumbs to its cryptanalytic pressure.

The Insecurity of Ad-Hoc Cyber Security

The cryptographic solutions to achieving a secure channel in the unsecured Internet are often misinterpreted. Once we examine the solutions described, we will conclude that they allow two parties who call themselves Alice and Bob to build a private channel in cyberspace, and use this channel with high degree of confidence. But there is nothing in these protocols that would ascertain to Alice that she talks to Bob, and not to David, or ascertain to Bob that he talks with Alice, and not with Carla. In other words, Ralph Merkle, Diffie–Hellmann, and RSA are means to establish privacy between two parties, whoever these parties are. Once Alice and Bob find some means to ascertain their mutual identities, then these privacy tools will do their jobs. This vulnerability opens the door for the man-in-the-middle (MiM) attack.

Man-in-the-Middle Fraud

Man-in-the-middle (MiM) is perhaps the most potent tool in the arsenal of security invaders. It allows Harry the Hacker to position himself undetectably between Alice and Bob as they converse in cyberspace. Harry reads everything that passes between Alice and Bob, and he can pounce at the opportune moment.

As we have seen before, the powerful privacy tools that we use to establish privacy between two strangers on the Internet are vulnerable to identity theft. Indeed suppose Alice wishes to establish a private channel with Bob so that she can securely exchange payment information with him. She goes on cyberspace and calls Bob. Harry the hacker intercepts this call and responds saying: "Hello Alice, I am Bob!" Alice connects. Soon after Harry calls Bob, pretending to be Alice, and connects with Bob who innocently believes he linked with Alice. Now even suppose that Alice and Bob are not strangers, they have communicated before, so Alice uses this fact to fend off hackers, and she asks Bob when was there last communication session. Harry the hacker, the man-in-the-middle (MiM) does not know the answer, and if he guesses it, and is wrong (most likely) then Alice will become suspicious of his true identity. But Harry does not need to guess, he simply turns to Bob and relays Alice's question to him. Bob's answer is then relayed back to Alice. Bob, on his part, may also be apprehensive, and ask Alice what dress did she wear in the conference last month. Harry relays the question to Alice, and then relays Alice's answer to Bob. In short, Harry's presence in the middle remains totally invisible both to Alice and to Bob despite their aggressive attempts to ascertain who they are talking to. Neither Alice nor Bob will suspect the eavesdropping of Harry because all their tests for each other are successful. They can exchange nonrepeating passwords, use any graphic identification, resort to any deep intimate familiarity they may have, this MiM invasion stubbornly remains undetected.

Any information Alice passed to Bob like her payment card, personal attributes, bank accounts – are all now in the possession of Harry the hacker, and will be exploited by him to clear out Alice's account. This is the fundamental weakness of account-based payment, the prevailing method for life in cyber space. This weakness is also a fundamental security reason for upgrading payment to e-cash modality that bears the means to defeat the MiM attack.

MiM vs. Digital Cash Payment

Since we concluded that Harry the hacker may establish himself between Alice and Bob while remaining invisible, we may now follow a payment session between Alice and Bob as Alice sends money to Bob. Alice will request Bob to send her his public key. Alice will concatenate that key to the coin and sign or encrypt the combined string with her private key, then send it all to Bob.

Bob will decrypt the package using Alice's public key, and will do what Alice did, when he wishes to transfer the coin further to Carla. When he does so, he signs the now longer coin package (that contains Carla's public key) by using his private key. Carla will use Bob's public key to decrypt Bob's encryption or signature, then use Alice's public key to decrypt her coin package, and then compare Bob's public key as it is written in Alice's signed package, to Bob's public key that she uses to decrypt his signature. If the two keys don't match – the coin is a fraud. Since the MiM never sees neither Bob's nor Alice's private key, he cannot exploit his knowledge of all that transpires between these two to steal the money.

What Harry can do, is to claim that he is Bob and use his pair of private/public keys to claim the money. In a decentralized currency this will work perfectly because the pair of keys is the only way to associate money to its owner. In a centralized trading environment, the mint will issue Bob an identity certificate to prove his ownership of his claimed public key.

We conclude then that the fundamental vulnerability of account-based payment – the MiM – is favorably handled in a digital cash environment, defeating fraud, waste, and abuse.

PRINTED DIGITAL COINS

Since the value of digital coins is expressed through the identities of their bits, they will carry their value on printed paper where bar code or any other code will be used to convey the digital string. Traders will be able to print out their money, hand it over as good currency, to be verified by the recipient upon scanning and reading the coin into electronic form.

PREPAID TRANSACTIONS

Their roots are old and their practice common: whether gift cards, or concert tickets, or a retainer pay to your lawyer, the idea of paying ahead of receiving the intended merchandise, or the agreed upon service, is implemented with great versatility and fashion. What drives this practice? The service provider surely loves it – payment is assured, float is collected; in many cases, interchange fee not paid —— no down side!

From the payer's point of view the picture is more complex. Generally speaking, a payer will find it advantageous to hold his money completely fungible until the moment of the transaction. Prepaying is prelimiting the funds; it amounts to losing spending flexibility, losing potential interest. Why bother? Looking deeper into this market it becomes clear that in many instances the payer is not the owner of the prepaid funds. A third party has a role in the scheme: gift cards are paid by the gift giver, and used by the gift receiver; food-stamps (EBT) are paid by the tax payer, and used by the benefits recipients. For the source of the money, the "prepaid" option is a clear advantage – it provides a guarantee that the money is spent as intended by the giver. Prepaid money so paid is regarded as tethered money: money that can be used only in accordance with well-defined terms. We have seen in previous sections that the most impactful attribute of digital money is it being so naturally tethered to a particular owner, to a particular use, to a set time frame, etc. This agreement in form suggests a functional marriage between digital money technology and prepaid money practice.

In 2003, $1 billion were prepaid into general-purpose cards. In 2012, the number was 65 times higher (source: CFPB). This surely does not represent a flash of generosity of third-party payers. These numbers reflect a clear and present advantage to regular payers. The main driver behind this surge is the growing economy of the unbanked, the underbanked, and the privacy conscious, as well as the soaring market for loyalty money, reward points, and coupons. The networks have quickly realized this trend and now offer reloadable cards that can be paid in cash, but used in cyberspace, side by side with the common well-banked credit card. Government regulators also see this trend, and newly devised regulations are coming forth to protect the prepaid consumer.

Much has been mentioned about the clear advantages of prepaid transactions with respect to security and privacy. And as mega breaches of millions of credit cards keep happening, the prepaid advantage soars to prominence. Is there a profound conclusion here waiting to be drawn? Come to think about it, the greenback started as "prepaid gold" before it evolved to a currency form in its own right. The difference was that at least theoretically paper dollars were completely reversible to chunks of gold. With the modern abundance of prepaid devices, we do have limited reversibility (general-purpose prepaid cards will allow cash withdrawal in ATM), but in general these schemes are irreversible. Let us turn them into completely reversible form of money. This will remove the psychological barrier from purchasing them.

And we need another adjustment: make prepaid more versatile, more ad-hoc, and increasingly frictionless. Case in point: Thrown off my bike, I had my shoulder fractured, and my doctor sent me to pose for X-ray. I filled up the paperwork for my insurer to postpay. Instead my insurer could have prepaid by sending a digital payment code to my phone, allowing me to shop for a place that would throw in a physiotherapy session for that pay. This is ad hoc, it would be impractical to issue a card for that purpose. Also, a digital payment code can include all the applicable terms and restrictions – fused cryptographically. It is then texted to my phone, and I text it off to the medical facility. Reversibility combined with tethering prepaid money to an owner (using a pair of private/ public keys, or a full name), when applied in conjunction with a smartphone, will do away with the myriad of prepaid cards, with the assortments of prepaid vehicles, and once it penetrates in full, it will turn the phone into our checking account, protected against theft and loss using the cryptographic equivalent of the old travelers checks. Now stop and evaluate: What is prepaid in the form of a digital payment string? It is digital currency! Not bitcoin which defies the

US dollars, and fluctuates in value, but more like fiat-extended digital currency that simply reformats the old greenback into a sequence of bits – easy to store, easy to pay, easy to crypto-secure – the future of money.

HYBRID COINS

Tangible, jingling coins, have been a part of the human experience for over a millennia. The drachma of Aegina was perhaps the earliest government stamped coin, minted in 700 BC and we have been tossing and counting them ever since.

Technology today offers a bridge and a continuity of habit with respect to these old-fashioned coins, while at the same time usher in the digital currency. Digital coin can be written on small-size electronic media that, in turn, would be encapsulated in an enclosure reminiscent of an old fashioned coin, or a modern replacement thereto. The only way to open this enclosure will be to "crack it open" like cracking an eggshell, so that one could not remove the electronic media from within, and then rebuild the enclosure as if it were still virgin. Such physical coins – hybrid coins – can be issued in any denomination. When people start trading with them, they would naturally be apprehensive, immediately crack open each received coin, and upload its internal media electronically validating its worth with the mint. But over time, based on experience, trust will be established, and traders will exchange these coins in their virgin states, with full confidence that they contain their denominated value in electronic digital form.

Accompanying Essays

A BRIEF HISTORY OF CRYPTOGRAPHY

Julius Caesar hid his messages by replacing every letter with the third letter down, hopping back to A after he reached Z. It served him well as history shows. Some of his contemporaries simply mixed letters in a word, then in a sentence, to achieve the same purpose. What Caesar did is called "substitution" – substituting one letter with one or more others. Letter mixing is called "transposition" – using the same letters in a different order. Cryptography underwent many changes ever since, but surprisingly these two basic operations, substitution and transposition, which are called primitives, have remained with us until this very day. If you pry open the workhorse of modern cryptography, that is, Advanced Encryption Standard (AES), or its predecessor, Data Encryption Standard (DES), you see a series of substitutions and transpositions following each other to create sufficient complexity to hinder a successful unknotting of the apparently meaningless gibberish we call ciphertext. A ciphertext is a message protected by our choice algorithm designed to resist all attempts to extract the plaintext out of it. We practiced a complex array of substitutions and transposition by hand before the computer era, alas our adversaries also used pencil and paper trying to crack our messages. After World War II we applied computers; our ciphers became much stronger, but so did our nemeses, and their cryptanalysis became much more effective too. Cat and mouse chase with dire consequences. America entered into World War I on account of a German cable cracked and decrypted by the British. The Nazis would have survived longer, had Alan Turing and his team in Bletchley Park not triumphed over the German Enigma cipher.

But today the stakes are immensely higher. Cryptography is no longer the exclusive domain of generals, politicians, and unfaithful spouses; it has loomed to become the foundation of modern life on cyberspace. The crypto industry flourishes: new ciphers pop up daily, but we use only a few, because we are afraid to employ an untrustworthy cipher. Cryptographers, like all of us, try to downplay embarrassing reality: none of the mainstay ciphers we use today are proven mathematically to be good for their declared purpose. We certify a cipher for heavy-duty applications on account of a test in which we commission someone to try and crack it, and regard a failure as proof of efficacy. Left unmentioned is the disturbing premise that this test is only valid if we are lucky enough and the people we try to protect it against are dumber than the people we commissioned to conduct the test. Why disturbing? Because we have no way of

Tethered Money: Managing Digital Currency Transactions. http://dx.doi.org/10.1016/B978-0-12-803477-4.00013-2
135

knowing whether an Alan Turing-like mind was born "over there" a quarter of a century ago, and now is doing to us what Turing did to Nazi Germany.

And what makes this well hidden and very disturbing secret of cryptography more amazing is the fact that almost hundred years ago, in 1917, a researcher at Bell Labs NJ, Gilbert S. Vernam, had patented a cipher, which Claude Shannon later proved to be unbreakable: not by a commissioned test, but by the full rigor and credibility of a mathematical proof. Using Vernam cipher incurred great inconvenience so we dropped it. The Russians picked it, and used it to siphon away the atomic secrets to Stalin. The FBI and the NSA have the ciphertexts, but can't decipher the messages until today!

When the Internet emerged, it connected strangers all over the globe, and where people go, commerce comes, and commerce operates on money; money attracts thieves, and requires protective countermeasures. But online, the only way to protect assets is by encryption. Encryption, since its inception, required a shared secret key (some string of data) between the writer and the reader. A random buyer and a random seller had no shared key. They could not practice encryption, nor carry out any online transaction without exposing their financial vitals to online fraudsters. But then, during 1970s, some young bright cryptographers like Merkle, Diffie, Hellmann, Rivest, Shamir and Adelman, invented an intellectual feat that opened the door to e-commerce, allowing two strangers to converse and pay discreetly, guarded by cryptography. Alas, the Vernam cipher cannot work here, and hacking is a looming danger.

The algorithmic invention of Rivest, Shamir and Adelman, better known as RSA, has found new usages. It allows people to sign a contract electronically. President Clinton signed it into law. It started an industry of identity certification, and provided means to protect against identity theft, and message contamination. RSA, when exposed mathematically, relies on the assumed difficulty to reverse multiplication of $x \times y = z$. For z sufficiently large, reverse extracting x, and y (if they are the only options) is considered a hard problem. Is it? Will it remain so? Are we betting against innovation? The Ralph Merkle solution, and similar ones, rely on probability and are not vulnerable to superior mathematical intellect. When applied to money such more robust cryptography is clearly more attractive, even though it may be less elegant.

Modern cryptography has mushroomed out to account for far away challenges like mistrustful collaboration, and towards tailored data exposure. For example, how to expose a database for analytics without violating the privacy rights of those whose data is being analyzed. But the "other shoe to fall" is clearly quantum cryptography. It is based on the bizarre and noncommonsensical premises of quantum mechanics. It is being aggressively researched in a grand competition around the world, and when it comes through it will reshuffle cryptography like nothing before.

Developers of crypto money need to not only account to the present reality, but also meet the daunting challenge of intercepting the crypto climate of years to come.

CRYPTOGRAPHIC SIGNATURES

Financial cryptography makes frequent use of a cryptographic signature. Alice can sign a document by encrypting it with her RSA private key, as she releases her corresponding public key to Bob who wishes to satisfy himself that Alice signed the document. How will Bob satisfy himself?

Bob will have before him the plaintext, P, of the document to be signed; the ciphertext, C, of P which Alice signed with her private key, (which Bob does not have), and Alice's public key, which Alice handed to him. Bob will then use Alice's public key to decrypt the ciphertext C into its corresponding plaintext, P'. If P = P' then Bob will conclude that the ciphertext C was indeed generated from the plaintext before him. And since Alice is the only one in possession of her private key, this leads one to conclude that Alice has seen and approved the context of the document she signed.

While this sounds very elegant, it is not unbreakable. Much as old fashioned signatures are subject to forgery and foul play, so is the case here: what if Carla has secretly stolen, or otherwise secured the possession of Alice's private key, and applied it to sign a document that Alice never saw? What if Carla has presented herself as Alice, talking to Bob online, and given him her public key, claiming it to be Alice's? And lastly, what if RSA was cryptanalyzed, and Carla could extract Alice's private keys from her public key?

There is a more elegant way to affect a digital signature: hashing. Hashing is a process of producing a short string of bits that corresponds to a long string of bits. A good hash is a one-way function, namely it is very easy to produce a short string, S from a long list of bits, L. But the reverse is very intractable. Alice could therefore hash the document she intends to sign, and produce a small string of bits, which she would encrypt with her private key. Bob would decrypt her signature, and then hash the document. Bob will be satisfied that the document is authentic if its hash is the same as the decryption of Alice's signature. The idea being that it would be very difficult for a forger to write another document that will generate the same hash.

Bitcoin is employing a hash signature in its protocol, but not RSA, rather elliptic curves.

DANIEL – DIGITAL MONEY FRIENDLY CIPHER

Daniel is a cipher of great value for digital money, on account of being dually principled: with short keys it works very much like all erosive complexity ciphers but, as the keys become longer and longer, it gradually transforms to equivocation based cipher, and in its extreme application Daniel is as unbreakable as the Vernam cipher. This feat is possible because unlike all the mainstay ciphers today, Daniel works as easily with large keys as with small ones. By contrast, for virtually all other ciphers, when the key becomes larger the computational burden quickly becomes prohibitive.

The Daniel principle is that a trip can be described either by listing its successive destinations, or by naming the road sections from one destination to the other. Given a map and a starting point A, Alice can write a travel plan by writing in sequence the points to visit: go from A to B, then from B to C, etc. Bob, walking according to Alice's instructions, might choose instead to log the roads he took. So Bob will record X (the road from A to B), then Y (the road from B to C), then Z (the road from C to D), etc. Clearly, Alice's instructions "A, B, C, D…" describe the same trip as Bob's "X, Y, Z…". It is clear that given the map, Carla could take Alice's description, and translate it to Bob's description, and vice versa. Carla will see that road X leads from A to B, and road Y leads from B to C, etc. But, if David does not have the map, then he is clueless as to translating Alice's description (A, B, C) to Bob's description (X, Y, Z), or vice versa. *That's it.*

We can call Alice's description the plaintext, and Bob's description the corresponding ciphertext. Given the map – the key – anyone could use one description of the trip and deduce the other. But wanting the map (not having the key) will make it impossible to translate one trip description to the other.

Obviously, the larger the message, the longer the trip. If the map covers sufficiently large area, then the path may never repeat itself, and one could substitute the real map with any arbitrary one of same size, and no cryptanalyst will be the wiser. Such freedom to substitute cryptographic keys (maps) implies equivocation, durability, and deniability. If the map is a bit smaller, then some destinations will have to be revisited more than once. This fact makes it a bit trickier to replace the used map with an arbitrary one. And, if the map is so small that the pathway zigzags in it, then arbitrary replacement is out of the question, there is only one solution, and that solution is protected with erosive complexity. Whatever the case, the encryption and/or decryption process is proportional to the size of the message, not the size of the map (the key). The reason is explained through the statement that it takes the same time for someone to walk ten miles on a stretched road, as to walk ten miles while zigzagging in his backyard.

For more details, please consult US Patent #6,823,068.

Glossary

Algorithm A set of specified instructions to operate on input data, and produce output data. The instructions must be so specific that the output data is the same whenever, and by whomever the algorithm is applied.

Asymmetric Encryption Encryption where a sender and a receiver of a cryptographic message do not share the same key data.

Bank A financial services institution, which mediates between people who have money to be stored for future use, and people who have need for money for present use.

Bitcoin A decentralized digital money system where all users can mint digital coins of shifting value relative to fiat currencies (e.g., US dollar), and where digital coins base their ability to serve as money by relying on erosive cryptographic complexity.

BitMint A non-speculative centralized digital money system that represents US dollars, other fiat currencies, or any valuables, where the money integrity is based on durable equivocation and not on erosive complexity.

Central Bank A national institute endowed with measures of political independence to achieve its objective to keep the national currency stable and effective. Its main tool is the means to control the supply of the national currency.

Cipher A procedure to encrypt a message so that a key holder can readily un-encrypt it, and others cannot.

Coin Redemption Receiving the nominal dollar value, or the reference valuable of a digital coin, against delivery of that coin.

Complexity A state where a large number of factors are cross-involved such that a great deal of effort is required to understand the construction, or the operation, or unfolding of the state.

Cryptanalysis The art and science of overcoming cryptographic complexity or cryptographic equivocation by those who do not have the proper cryptographic key.

Cryptographic Complexity The complexity applied to hide a message such that those without a proper decryption key will not be able to understand the message in a timely manner.

Cryptographic Decryption Key A measure of data that enables its possessor to retrieve a message hidden through cryptography.

Cryptographic Encryption Key A measure of data that is used by its possessor to encrypt messages.

Cryptographic Equivocation A state where a cryptanalyst faces two or more possible and plausible messages such that each of them may be the object of the cryptanalysis, but there is no way to identify for certain which one is the message of interest.

Cryptography The art and science of injecting either complexity or equivocation into data so that only those who posses a key – a measure of data – can remove the complexity and/or the equivocation, and understand the intended message, while those without the key will not be able to retrieve the hidden message in a timely manner.

Tethered Money: Managing Digital Currency Transactions. http://dx.doi.org/10.1016/B978-0-12-803477-4.00015-6
139

Currency Wars A war where nations unilaterally manipulate the exchange rates of their currency to harm enemy nations.

Decryption A process of using a cryptographic key to recover the intended message from its encrypted form.

DigiCash A now defunct digital money system based on a process known as "blind signature" designed to achieve cash-like anonymity.

Digital Coin A measure of digital money.

Digital Money Money expressed as a string of bits where the string represents both value and identity of an entity that carries said value.

Encryption A process of applying cryptography to a message so that only its intended readers can understand it.

Erosive (Cryptographic) Complexity Cryptographic complexity that erodes with time, usually on account of (i) more effective computing machines, and (ii) deeper mathematical insight.

Loyalty Money Tethered money valid for purchasing items from specified vendors and no other.

Mint An entity that issues money.

Money Medium of economic exchange, a means to store value, and a unit of accounting.

Redemption see *Coin Redemption*

Secure Validation Delegation (SVD) A method to delegate the authority to validate digital coins.

Symmetric Encryption Encryption where a sender and a receiver of a cryptographic message share the same key data, or mutually deducible key data.

Tethered Money Money with built-in limitation on use.

Further Readings

Aaronson, S., et al., 2012. Quantum money. Commun. ACM 55 (8).

Aron, J., 2012. Virtual economy looms as digital cash grows up. New Scientist, November 2012.

Cajori, F., 1918. Pierre Laurent Wantzel. Bull. Am. Math. Soc. 24 (7), 339–347.

Gödel, K., 1931. On formally undecidable propositions of Principia Mathematica and related systems I. Monatshefte für Mathematik.

Hunton, P., 2012. Data attack of the cybercriminal: investigating the digital currency of cybercrime. Comput. Law Security Rev. 28 (2), 201–207, 7 p.

Ignacio, M., 2011. Smart banknotes. The Futurist. January, February 2011.

Jacobs, E., 2011. Bitcoin: a bit too far. JIBC.

Paganelli, M., 2012. What is money for. The Intercollegiate Review. Spring 2012.

Popescu, C., 2011. A secure e-cash transfer system based on the elliptic curve discrete logarithm problem. Informatica 22 (3), 395–409.

Rickards, J., 2011. Currency Wars: The Making of the Next Global Crisis. Portfolio & Penguin.

Samid, G., 2001. Anonymity management: a blue print for newfound privacy. The Second International Workshop on Information Security Applications, WISA 2001, Seoul, Korea, September 13–14, 2001 (Best Paper Award).

Samid, G., 2001. Encryption sticks (Randomats). ICICS 2001 Third International Conference on Information and Communications Security Xian. China, November 13–16, 2001.

Samid, G., 2001. Re-dividing complexity between algorithms and keys (key scripts). The Second International Conference on Cryptology in India. Indian Institute of Technology, Madras, Chennai, India, December 2001

Samid, G., 2002. At-will intractability up to plaintext equivocation achieved via a cryptographic key made as small, or as large as desired – without computational penalty. 2002 International Workshop on Cryptology and Network Security, San Francisco, California, USA, September 26–28, 2002.

Samid, G., 2002. Validity calculus: a novel methodology to manage high-uncertainty projects. AACE-I Proceedings, July 2002.

Samid, G., 2003. e-Identity: an unsolved problem. International Conference on Computer, Communication and Control Technologies, CCCT '03. Orlando, Florida, USA, July 31, August 1–2, 2003.

Samid, G., 2003. Intractability erosion: the everpresent threat for secure communication. The Seventh World Multi-Conference on Systemics, Cybernetics and Informatics, SCI 2003, July 2003.

Samid, G., 2003. Non-zero entropy ciphertexts (stochastic decryption): on the possibility of one-time-pad class security with shorter keys. 2003 International Workshop on Cryptology and Network Security, CANS03. Miami, Florida, USA, September 24–26, 2003

Samid, G., 2005. The myth of invincible encryption. Digital Transactions. May–June 2005.

Samid, G., 2006. The Innovation Turing Machine. DGS Vitco.

Tethered Money: Managing Digital Currency Transactions. http://dx.doi.org/10.1016/B978-0-12-803477-4.00016-8

Samid, G., 2007. Proposing a master one-way function. The International Association for Cryptologic Research, IACR, eprint October 3, 2007.

Samid, G., 2008. Encryption-on-demand: practical and theoretical considerations. The International Association for Cryptologic Research IACR, eprint May 16, 2008.

Samid, G., 2009. The Unending Cyberwar. DGS Vitco.

Samid, G., 2009. Innovation Solution Protocol Web-Wide Innovation, Picmet-09 (Oregon 2009). Passed Peer Review and Accepted.

Samid, A., 2010. Technology driven universal currency. United Nations Commission on Science and Technology for Development.

Samid, G., 2010. Knowledge realization momentum. International Conference on Information and Knowledge Engineering, IKE'11 2010.

Samid, G. Bit currency: transactional trust tools. US Patent #8,229,859.

Samid, G. Denial cryptography based on graph theory. US Patent #6,823,068.

Schiff, P., 2012. The Real Crash: America's Coming Bankruptcy – How to Save Yourself and Your Country. St. Martin Press.

Srivastava, S., 2012. E-cash payment protocols. IJCSE.

Turing, A., 1936. On computable numbers, with an application to the Entscheidungs problem. Proceedings of the London Math Society 2nd Ser., 42 m, pp. 230–265.

US Congress Hearing, 2006. Coin and currency issues facing Congress: can we still afford money. Hearing Before the Subcommittee on Domestic and International Monetary Policy, Trade, and Technology of the Committee on Financial Services U.S. House of Representatives One Hundred Ninth Congress Second Session, July 19, 2006.

Van den Berg, H.F., 2012. Technology, complexity, and culture as contributors to financial instability: a generalization of Keynes's Chapter 12 and Minsky's financial instability hypothesis. J. Econ. Issues.

Index

About the Author

Prof Gideon Samid, PhD, PE specializes in cyber security, cryptography, artificial intelligence, engineering design, and the general theory of innovation. He serves as the Chief Technology Officer for BitMint, LLC, and for AGS Encryptions Ltd. His recent focus is designing a comprehensive framework for global digital currency – banking and payment: cryptographic protocols, online and offline payment interchange, and chemical cryptography. Prof Samid writes a monthly column for Digital Transactions magazine. He has authored critically acclaimed technology books, such as "The Dawn of Digital Currency," "The Unending Cyberwar," "Computer-Organized Cost Engineering," and "The Innovation Turing Machine" as well as dozens of peer-reviewed technical articles. Prof. Samid teaches cyber security, financial cryptography, and digital money technology, offered through Case Western Reserve University, and through the University of Maryland, UC. His interactive online course (WeSecure.net/learn) has over 110,000 visitors, students. He is a researcher at the Department of Electrical Engineering and Computer Science, Case Western Reserve University. Prof Samid earned his three academic degrees at the Technion – Israel Institute of Technology. He claims several pending patents and has been granted two US patents for equivocation-based cryptography, and for secure digital money transactions. Gideon Samid charted a broad engineering career spanning computer science, chemical engineering, nuclear engineering, and control engineering, working for several government agencies, and in the private sector (e.g., NASA, Exxon, Presearch, SAC), and he was managing an engineering boutique (D&G Sciences) specializing in innovation productivity, and applied engineering mathematics. His book "Unbound Ignorance" describes the author's theory of knowledge and scientific inquiry. Gideon and Dolores jointly enjoy their wonderful families.

Made in the USA
Lexington, KY
17 February 2016